Mormons
in Transition

Mormons in Transition

Second Edition

Leslie Reynolds

BakerBooks

A Division of Baker Book House Co
Grand Rapids, Michigan 49516

© 1996, 1998 by Leslie Reynolds

Published by Baker Books
a division of Baker Book House Company
P.O. Box 6287, Grand Rapids, MI 49516-6287

First edition published by Gratitude Press

Printed in the United States of America

Library of Congress Cataloging-in-Publication Data

Reynolds, Leslie, 1941–
    Mormons in transition / Leslie Reynolds.—2nd ed.
      p.   cm.
    Includes bibliographical references.
    ISBN 0-8010-5811-2 (pbk.)
    1. Mormons—United States—Religious life. 2. Church of Jesus Christ of Latter-Day Saints—Membership. 3. Ex-church members—Church of Jesus Christ of Latter-Day Saints. 4. Church work with ex-church members—Church of Jesus Christ of Latter-Day Saints. 5. Mormon Church—United States—Membership. 6. Mormon Church—Controversial literature. I. Title.
BX8656.R45   1998
289.3—dc21   97-53293

For current information about all releases from Baker Book House, visit our web site:
http://www.bakerbooks.com

For the man I met in June 1991 at a Del Taco on Del Amo and Hawthorne Boulevards in Torrance, California. I'm sorry to have lost your card, because you gave me my life. My deepest thanks.

Contents

Preface to the Second Edition

Since I strongly believe that this book carries a valuable message not only for those Christians interested in understanding Mormonism but also for those interested in witnessing to Mormons, I was pleased when Baker Book House agreed to publish this revised edition of *Mormons in Transition*. While I had success with the first edition, I lacked access to the Christian market outside Utah, parts of Idaho, and a single city in Arizona.

I believe this book to be valuable also to former Mormons who now follow Jesus Christ as revealed in the Bible. It can take years for former Mormons to fully acclimate to traditional Christian churches, and I believe that this book is helpful in relieving their pain, confusion, and loneliness.

Additionally, I have found much success with this book as an evangelistic tool, not for the temple-recommend-carrying died-in-the-wool Mormons,[1] but for those among the millions of questioning or disaffected Mormons who may or may not still practice Mormonism. We, the readers of *Mormons in Transition,* need to understand that for many of them, Mormonism is an identity rather than a religion, and if we attack that identity, they will strike a defensive posture and end up distrusting us. Many of them are silently crying, "Please don't attack us. You just don't understand."

It is hard for them to see that it is their eyes that are closed to understanding. Be gentle with them. I know.

Many people have asked for my story. It's unconventional but it may be typical for a former Mormon. I wandered through Eastern religions, self-actualization seminars, and the New Age movement, with three dips back into the Latter-day Saints (Mormon) church before accepting Jesus as my Lord and Savior at the age of fifty. Apparently, I threw Jesus out with Joseph Smith when I uncovered what I describe as the myth of Mormonism.[2]

My problems with the LDS church began in the mid-1950s, when I was thirteen or fourteen. I was bright and asked questions about belief and doctrine—very real questions for me. This questioning was not accepted. Finally, in 1955, I was denied attendance at the seminary (daily religion classes held each weekday morning), of which I had been elected president, for what amounted to trusting Jesus more than the current prophet (president of the LDS church). While continuing to attend church, I lost my evangelical zeal. I left the church at the age of sixteen when my family moved a short distance to a new, assigned congregation.

I read *No Man Knows My History*[3] in 1963 and, with that reading, thought I had settled the issue of my relationship to the LDS church. I firmly thought I was out. Then in 1967, I was surprised when my husband converted to the LDS church, and I was even more surprised to find myself pleased! All my previous rational arguments went out the window because I now had an opportunity to be sealed to him and to my two children in the LDS temple.[4] I could take my rightful place as an adult in the community of Salt Lake City. With the completion of my husband's doctorate in 1968, however, we moved to North Carolina, and within a year or so we drifted away from church attendance.

In 1970 we moved to California, and I began searching for something to fill the hole created when I left Mormonism. I also began to develop symptoms of the disease of alcoholism. My recovery from that disease led me back to the LDS church in 1981 for about a year and again in 1989 for a year and a half, as I tried to resolve troubling theological and social issues for myself. I so badly wanted an official stamp of approval. I wanted the Mormon dream, but I couldn't reconcile the LDS god with the big, broad, powerful, in-charge God I had come to accept.

Praise the Lord, I had a conversion experience while walking back to my office in 1991, but I didn't realize the significance at the time. I thought, *Oh, I have some catching up to do,* and I started attending a local Catholic church where a close friend was a priest. God opened my eyes to unethical practices, and within six months I closed my psychotherapy practice in California and moved back to Salt Lake City.

I started investigating churches—casually. Then, as Utah was preparing a racially motivated execution of a black man, a convicted accomplice to murder, who had left the scene of the crime before the murders were committed, I found myself attending nightly prayer vigils at the governor's mansion with many local Christian leaders. After this man was executed, I attended a memorial service for him at a local predominantly African American Baptist church, where I later discovered the racism in my own background and communicated those painful incidents to the pastor of that church, who is the leader of the black community in Salt Lake. I also asked him if I could visit his church. Within a few months, I accepted the call to be baptized in that congregation.

I remained in that congregation for a couple of years, attended seminary at Regent College in Vancouver, B.C.,[5] wrote the first edition of this book, and now find myself wandering among churches again. I have long practiced a morning meditation that now includes Bible reading. I find that I need daily communal prayer as well, so I attend one

11

church daily for morning prayer and another for Sunday services.

After discovering that a large, local psychiatric hospital offered only LDS services to its patients, I have been privileged to lead two weekly worship services there, one in the closed unit and one in the dining room. I want to provide the patients with an alternative to Mormonism.

I thank God daily for the richness of my life in Christ but still occasionally ask him, "Are you certain this is my correct course?" or "Is Mormonism really just a fiction of Joseph Smith?" May those who read this book and who don't know the answer to this second question ask the Lord to show them the truth and find the peace and contentment I now have with Jesus Christ as my Lord, Savior, and closest friend.

Preface to the First Edition

As a former counselor specializing in helping families affected by alcoholism and other addictions or compulsions, I often used the metaphor of the elephant in the living room:

There is a giant elephant sitting right in the middle of the living room, and everyone pretends that it is not there. Instead, they develop coping behaviors, rationalizations, explanations, and defenses against any mention of there being an elephant in the living room. They learn to walk around it, over it, and into it, but they never acknowledge its existence.

There is an elephant in the living room of Mormon country. That elephant is systematically ignored or pretended away. But it still exists. And denying its existence is as painful and self-destructive as alcoholic drinking or practicing any other addiction. The elephant is comprised of members of the LDS church who are losing their faith in the tenets of their church or leaving active church participation. These events go on all the time, but rarely are they talked about openly in the community. Members who doubt the veracity of their church's teachings tend to keep their questions to themselves. Their private thoughts tend to become secret thoughts and fears. And secrets invariably do damage.

So the mental health of the community demands that it acknowledge the elephant sitting right in the middle of the living room. There are numbers of active LDS church members who no longer believe but attend merely to maintain appearances for business, political, social, or family reasons. There are questioners who feel guilty for even daring to ask. There are people who quit attending who are ostracized from not only neighborhood and social groups but business groups. The pressure is strong to remain in "the church," as the Church of Jesus Christ of Latter-day Saints is called in Mormon country.

Former Mormons will find this book useful as a clarification of their process of leaving the church. Inactive Mormons, too, will find it useful to gain perspective on what it means to be a Mormon and possibly to aid in completing their experience of the LDS church. This book may also be a resource for questioning Mormons, to let them know how others like themselves have resolved their questions. Friends of all of these will find this book an aid in understanding and supporting their friends. Newcomers to Mormon country unfamiliar with the LDS church can use this book to gain perspective on the differences between the teachings of the LDS church and traditional Christian churches. And traditional Christian pastors will find this book useful in understanding the Mormon worldview, in assisting those struggling with the process of transition, and in supporting the assimilation of their former-Mormon congregants.

It is my earnest hope and prayer that this book will contribute to the healing of the community by acknowledging the elephant in the living room.

Acknowledgments

First, I thank the lady, who asked to remain anonymous, whose letter inspired this book.

And also those interviewed who cared to use their real names: Tim Schmall, Russ Lane, Cindy Lou Blackmon, Sandra Tanner, Will McGarvey, Niki Payne, Karen Clark, Alyce Covey, Larry DuBois, Bryan Ohlsen, Ross Anderson, Tawna Robinson, Christine Campbell, Brittany Fyans, Lynda Cooley, Evah Bigler. And the pastors: Chris Vlachos, Bill Heersink, Jeff Silliman, Dave Heikkela, and Pat Edwards.

And my readers: Chris Nelson, Diane Gooch, Gail McCulloch, Ed Firmage, Dave Rowe, Chris Vlachos, Mary Dern, Dee Ann Raynor, Karen, and Pat Pitcher, whose criticisms were essential to the accuracy of this book.

Ken Mulholland of UIBS and James Houston of Regent College, who supported me in writing my ministry research project. The faculty of both those schools where I began my theological retraining process. Tom McClenahan for countless private hours of instruction and editorial support on the second edition.

Alan Smith, Ardean Watts, Allan Roberts, Marilyn Banks, and Ghena Dalby for their helpful conversations. Bill Siefrit, friend, professional associate, and fellow author for recommending people to be interviewed.

My mother, Barbara Reynolds, for renting me an apartment for one hundred dollars per month plus yard work, without which I would have been unable to research and write this manuscript.

Robb Benns, my prayer partner, handyman, movie companion, and best friend.

My sister-in-law, Joanne Poon, for design, composition, and moral support on the first edition.

My brother, Rodger Reynolds, for his freely given editorial support on this manuscript, as well as others in the past. And also for his production guidance and legwork on the first edition. Rodger, I thank you for helping me to say what I thought I was saying. There's nothing like having publishers in the family.

To Baker Book House, and especially Dan Van't Kerkhoff, senior editor, for considering this manuscript.

Introduction

This project was born in the summer of 1994. After putting on a very successful Christian Institute for Mormon Studies jointly with Sandra Tanner,[1] the Utah Institute for Biblical Studies[2] received an angry letter from a former-Mormon participant who was struggling to make the transition from the LDS church to traditional Christianity. Ken Mulholland, the president of UIBS said, "It's too bad we don't have a book to give them [Mormons in the process of leaving]." I volunteered to write one.

My plan was to write a book that would give Mormons in the process of leaving the LDS church an opportunity to identify their situation. They could read it and say, "Oh, I see, I'm somewhere between steps two and three" and know that they were experiencing what others had before them, thereby easing some of their anxiety, anger, and pain. I researched the books in publication and discovered that none did the job. One book that might have performed that function, *Out of the Cults and into the Church* by Janis Hutchinson, was published in September 1994. Mormons, however, do not identify with belonging to a cult.[3] So her book, no matter how good, would probably never reach the hands of people who might benefit from reading it.[4]

In the fall of 1994, I needed a ministry research project for a master's degree in Christian studies at Regent College in Vancouver, B.C. For the project, and as an aid to writing the book I had committed to complete, I chose to determine the specific steps that Mormons take in leaving the LDS church and the attendant LDS worldview and coming to traditional Christianity.

If you are a little suspicious or put off at any mention of organized religion or traditional Christianity, as many former LDS church members are, please relax. I wrote this book first as a therapist and second as a fairly new convert (five years) to traditional Christianity. Leaving the comfort of the LDS church causes, in most, a spiritual crisis. I believe that a spiritual problem requires a spiritual solution, in the same way that a medical problem requires a medical solution. And, believe me, losing faith in your religion can result in a spiritual crisis, even though you don't recognize it as such.

Methodology

For the master's degree project, I interviewed thirteen former Mormons (see questionnaire in appendix B) who now identify themselves as traditional Christians, and five traditional Christian pastors. (I actually interviewed a sixth pastor, Ross Anderson, but he is considered a former Mormon here.) After completing my degree, I conducted other interviews to broaden my responses beyond those obtained from people who define themselves as non-Mormon Christians. I interviewed seven others who still consider themselves Mormons but are not fully believing, active members.

Those whom I interviewed live and work along the geographical spine of the LDS church's strength, Utah's Wasatch front, extending one hundred miles from Ogden, located north of Salt Lake, to Provo, on the south. The LDS church is a culture as well as a religious body. It is frequently described from LDS pulpits as a "way of life." And there are many Mormons who have little more than a nodding acquaintance with the religious principles of their faith. They are referred to as "cultural" Mormons. The pastors interviewed all had former Mormons in their congregations.

The former Mormons I interviewed for my degree project ranged in age from twenty-one to sixty. Eight were women and five were men. They had been out of the church for three and a half to thirty-four years. They had left active participation in the church at ages ranging from thirteen to fifty. The sampling of former Mormons shows an even distribution of both age at time of interview and time away from active participation in the LDS church. Since I had chosen my interviewees intuitively and not analytically, I was surprised that I ended up with such a wide distribution.

All but one of these respondents had become firmly convinced that the doctrines of the LDS church were false. Each of the former Mormons (as distinct from questioning or inactive Mormons) now professes to be a traditional Christian, to have a personal relationship with Jesus, and each acknowledges him as God and personal Savior.

The acknowledged purpose of my research project was to identify the steps that people go through in leaving the LDS church. In this research, not only did I interview former Mormons but I reviewed the material of other researchers, most importantly that of Laura M. Marwick,[5] a Brigham Young University student (see appendix C). I found many well researched and documented theories about the steps that people go through in leaving a cult, the LDS church, or other similar churches.

Results

My hands-on research led me to a different conclusion than I had originally expected. With the small and less than random sample I interviewed, I found that while there was some similarity in their processes, each individual moved in what appeared to be an almost random fashion through various attitudes and conditions. They did not take common, identifiable, sequential steps. The workings of God did not fit into the descriptive systems designed by this limited human being.

The seven respondents I interviewed who still identify themselves as Mormons cannot be described as content with their faith. It did not occur to me to interview active Mormons for this book, though I have several active, believing Mormon friends, some of whom volunteered to read this manuscript. All of those interviewed had indicated that, while still being Mormon, they were less than active, temple-worthy members. However, one of those interviewed is currently attending the LDS church and is seeking a temple recommend. I picked these potential respondents for their diversity in beliefs and experiences. They encompass cultural, social, and heterodox Mormons. Once again, I picked my respondents intuitively. My question to these people was much more general than to the Christian converts. I asked only, "Tell me about your relationship with the Mormon church." Four of the seven members of this last group requested anonymity.

I had planned to write a treatise documenting the steps that Mormons go through in leaving the LDS church, but my research showed that people didn't follow linear steps in a 1, 2, 3 fashion.[6] I have, instead, anecdotal information from former and still questioning Mormons on several important issues, in which they share their experiences and reasons for changing position in relationship to the LDS church. Short biographical notes about respondents at the time they were interviewed are scattered throughout the book.

Purpose

Leaving the LDS church can be painful. As both a former Mormon and a former psychotherapist who has suffered a painful crisis of faith, I intend this book to help former Mormons in various levels of pain to heal and to help others, both Mormon and non-Mormon, gain perspective on the LDS church and their experiences with it. One of my respondents quoted a study purportedly carried out by the LDS church that leads me to believe that 75 percent of all baptized Mormons stop attending church for a while.[7] My assumption is that many of those inactive members are suffering as I have, and they may still be. I intend this book to help answer the questions that may have led to their inactivity and soothe their possible guilt and/or shame for leaving the LDS church. Maybe something here will ring true for them.

Although my point of view is that of a practicing biblical Christian, my intention is neither to cajole, nor lecture, nor preach. I believe that our pain can be most easily relieved by listening to others and looking for ways to identify with them. There is power in that identification.

For those who think this book might be an anti-Mormon tract, and you consider yourself a defender of the church, I'd like to cite the text that follows the famous "burning-in-the-bosom" scripture from the *Doctrine and Covenants*: "But if it is not right, you shall have no such feelings, but you shall have such a stupor of thought that shall cause you to forget the thing which is wrong" (9:9).[8] In other words, this passage says that you would not be harmed by continuing to read this book, because if it is wrong you will forget the things you read.

For some this book will be painful, for some enlightening. Some may find freedom in this book, and some a completion of their experience. It is my prayer that no matter what your experience, reading it will serve you.

21

1

Traditional Christianity versus Mormonism

The Utah Institute for Biblical Studies received a letter from a woman who had attended UIBS's biannual Christian Institute for Mormon Studies conference. The correspondent appeared to be very angry[1] (see appendix A for complete text of letter). As a former Mormon myself, I could feel the pain beneath her anger—the pain of being lost without a grounding organization for guidance. Another former Mormon, Janis Hutchinson, describes this painful situation where the individual "is suddenly aware that slipping away is a culture that defined who he or she was and what his or her role in life was."[2] Loss of such guidance is not merely a crisis of faith but one of identity as well. The writer of the letter had asked three questions to presenters at the CIMS conference to which she felt she had received unsatisfactory answers:

1. From whence comes your authority?
2. Why is it superior to/greater than that of Mormonism?
3. Why are there so many widely (WILDLY) varied Christian churches? How do you identify the "real thing"?

The letter writer adds an additional question, and then details her complaints with the answers she received:

> To which I add one more: "Because of the disparities and variances in the churches of the Christian realm, WHO HAS and WHAT IS the REAL TRUTH? HOW CAN I KNOW FOR ABSOLUTE CERTAIN?" I received what I felt was rather a non-answer to question #1: "That he was 'CHOSEN' and given 'SPECIAL GIFTS AND TALENTS.'" Come on now!

And she detailed her frustration with a lack of answers.

> In my mind, GOD'S TRUTH IS CONSTANT! IT IS UNCHANGING BECAUSE IT IS ETERNAL TRUTH! IT DOES NOT WAIVER [sic]! IT WOULD NOT VARY FROM ONE RELIGION TO ANOTHER, OR EVEN FROM ONE CONGREGATION TO ANOTHER WITHIN THE SAME RELIGION! I am sorry, but the disparities and wide variances in the Christian churches makes [sic] me NUTS!

The author of the letter was looking for a replacement true church and despaired of the diversity of traditional Christian beliefs.

> It seems to me that NONE have it right or there would not be the disparities and variances between Christian religions, and even between congregations within the same religion! GOD'S TRUTH DOES NOT CHANGE ACCORDING TO THE WHIMS OF A GROUP OR A CERTAIN PASTOR!

She goes on to explain that her problem is additionally complicated by her own state of mind. "Since leaving Mormonism, feeling so horribly DUPED AND BETRAYED! I have been very wary of organized religion in all its forms."

Latayne Scott, an author who is a former Mormon, came to an even more cynical conclusion: "I was convinced that if there was no God in the Mormon Church, then there was no god anywhere! I mean, if the LDS beliefs weren't true, there could be nothing else."[3]

The Crisis

To understand the depth of such a crisis requires a look at the tenets of the church itself. The LDS church, popularly called Mormonism, teaches that it is the one and only true church, that the truth was lost in a period of apostasy in the first century and was restored to the earth through the LDS prophet Joseph Smith. Smith gave the corrected dogma through revelation recorded as scripture. The power to discern the truth has been held, ever since, exclusively by the General Authorities of the LDS church.

People who leave the safety of such a defined dogma feel as though they are sailing without a rudder. When that guidance system fails, they need a strong validation that they are on the correct path. Since a spiritual crisis demands a spiritual solution, those believing in Jesus Christ can find their way again by moving their attention from what they have lost to developing a relationship with Jesus. In the meantime, they could also use the help of someone who has been where they are now, someone with compassion for the depth of their pain and confusion. For those who are not seeking a spiritual solution, problems can develop as they try to deny the crisis.

The LDS Church and Traditional Christianity

An Overview

A wide range of misunderstanding exists between Mormons (members of the Church of Jesus Christ of Latter-day Saints) and traditional Christians. As Presbyterian Pastor Jeff Silliman says, "There are semantic barriers to communication. We have a lot of words in common, but these words are understood one way in historical Christianity and another in their tradition." Words used by one group may offend the other.

For example, one Mormon I interviewed was offended because I referred to myself as a Christian, an acceptable designation in the traditional Christian culture, where we do not belong to a church, per se, but are followers of Christ and can worship in any denomination that suits us. He apparently believed I was claiming membership in *another* "one true church," albeit a different one from the LDS church. I know that Mormons consider themselves Christians, as I consider myself a Christian. However, we worship different Gods and acknowledge a different Jesus. Throughout this book, I will use the term *Christian* to refer to traditional Christians, or members of the historical body of Christ. These Christians are followers of Jesus, who is God, one with the Father, and they also acknowledge Jesus as their personal Savior.

I noticed in my interviews with people who identified themselves as Mormons that a majority of them thought they understood the beliefs of other churches. But as they started to explain these beliefs to me, most of them became aware that they do not. Over forty years ago I was taught that non-LDS churches were of the devil. This belief definitely limited my investigation into other denominations and their beliefs. Although this incorrect teaching of the past has apparently been altered to the position that "most religions have some truth," most of my respondents were ignorant of more traditional Christian beliefs and the differences with the LDS religion.

The LDS church and traditional Christianity have been at odds since Mormonism's inception. The LDS church calls traditional Christianity the result of a "Great Apostasy" (see *apostasy* in the glossary), while the traditional Christian is likely to call the LDS church a cult or a collection of well-known heresies with a twist—the anthropomorphizing of God. Traditional Christianity stresses that people are saved by grace alone through belief in Jesus Christ. Whereas, while Mormons believe in the mission of Jesus Christ as Savior of the world, they believe they can only be exalted through their own works. Frequently, traditional Christians are aghast at what they see in the LDS faith as a human physicality limiting their majestic God, while Mormons don't relate to a God of spirit, particularly one that is three beings in one—the Trinity. The LDS church has a godhead of three separate entities.

Historian Jan Shipps maintains that the LDS church is neither a Christian denomination nor a heresy, but something new. She asserts, "despite the surprising similarity between some of the modern cultural manifestations of Mormonism and American evangelical Protestantism, Mormonism started to grow away from traditional Christianity almost immediately upon coming into existence."[4] The group recognized Joseph Smith as a prophet of God, published new scriptures, restored the Aaronic priesthood (and later the Melchizedek priesthood), and instituted other traditions "that now distinguish their tradition from the Christian tradition as surely as early Christianity was distinguished from its Hebraic context."[5]

Another historian, Ruth A. Tucker, agrees: "The Mormon church is not merely a denomination that differs with other denominations on secondary or peripheral doctrines or practices; rather, it is a new religious movement which differs from Christianity on primary and essential doctrines and that stands alone with additional scriptures and beliefs that have never been a part of historic Christianity."[6] Yet another historian, Ken Mulholland, labels the LDS church as a specific culture, ". . . an *ethnos* [people] in a cultural sense, and they do have a very different way of conceptualizing truth than we do as Christians."[7]

It is not within the scope of this book to explain all the theological differences between the LDS church and traditional Christianity. I will, however, present a short introduction to the tenets of Mormonism for the reader who is not familiar with the church and its theology. I will then contrast Mormonism with historical Christianity. I refer the reader seeking further definition to this book's glossary, which gives more extensive definitions of the words that may be used in different ways by the LDS church and traditional Christianity. Doctrinal and cultural usages are also often listed there.

Theological Differences

The first major theological difference involves the LDS church's definition of God. While traditional Christian churches believe God to be three persons in the unity of one substance, or the Trinity, Mormons believe God is the "Eternal Father, the Father of Jesus Christ and of the spirits of all men."[8] They believe that Heavenly Father was once just like us—human, finite, and tempted by sin—but through right choices progressed to a more glorious level of being. Milton R. Hunter says, "Mormon prophets have continuously taught the sublime truth that God the Eternal Father was once a mortal man who passed through a school of earth similar to that through which we are passing. He became God—an exalted being." Charles W. Penrose states: "Mormonism does not tend to debase God to level of man, but to exalt man to the perfection of God."[9]

In the LDS church, the Father, Son, and Holy Ghost are three separate beings, two of which, the Father and the Son, have physical, albeit glorified, bodies. Jesus is the first-born spirit, begat of God and Heavenly Mother. He was born on earth to gain a body and conquer both spiritual and physical death, thereby leading the way for the rest of humankind. Jesus' endurance of the sins of mankind occurred in Gethsemane, causing him to bleed from every pore, according to the Mormon scripture (*Doctrine and Covenants* 19:18–19). He later experienced physical death on the cross.[10]

In the church's current desire to be accepted as a Christian religion ("How could anyone say we are not Christian? We have Christ's name in the name of our church."), Mormons have become slippery in answering direct questions. For example, in June 1997, Apostle M. Russell Ballard was interviewed on television and was asked the following question: "Do you believe that Jesus is God?" Ballard's answer was, "Well, yes. He is the *son* of God and a member of the godhead."[11]

According to the LDS church's *Gospel Principles*, "God is not only our ruler and our creator, he is also our Heavenly Father. . . . Every person who was born on earth was our spirit brother or sister in heaven. The first spirit born to our heavenly parents was Jesus Christ. He is our elder brother."[12] The book continues later to explain that "The Holy Ghost is a member of the Godhead. He has a body of spirit. His body of spirit is in the form of a man."[13]

Mormons also view their stay on earth as but one step in the process of eternal progression toward the celestial kingdom (the highest degree of glory in heaven). While born in the Spirit Kingdom, Mormons believe they come to earth to gain a body (see fig. 1). As is explained in *Gospel Princi-*

Figure 1

Mormon Plan of Eternal Progression

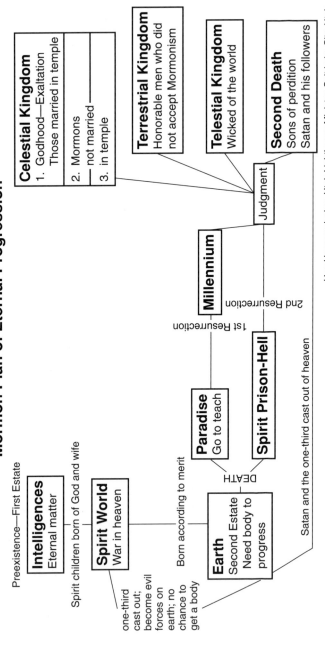

Used by permission, Utah Lighthouse Ministry, Salt Lake City, Utah

ples, "We are living for eternity and not just for the moment. However the blessings of eternal marriage can be ours now as well as for eternity. . . . Some of the blessings we can enjoy for eternity are: 1. We can live in the highest degree of the celestial kingdom of God. 2. We can be exalted as God is now exalted and receive a fullness of joy. 3. We can, at some future time, increase our family by having spirit children."[14]

Whereas most traditional Christian beliefs are vague concerning the afterlife, Christians hold that marriages do not exist in heaven and that Jesus is God and not our elder brother. Christians also do not believe that we have any potential for becoming gods of and populating our own worlds.

Two more major differences between Mormonism and traditional Christianity are the concepts of original sin and salvation. In the Mormon view, Adam and Eve were playing their assigned part in the eternal progression, their transgression is not related to our sinfulness, and "men will be punished for his own sins and not for Adam's transgression."[15] According to an analogy used by Boyd K. Packer in *Ensign* magazine and reprinted in *Gospel Principles,* humans must pay Christ back in full for his atoning sacrifice.[16] According to the LDS doctrine, the death of Jesus "makes it possible for us to overcome spiritual death. . . . We accept Christ's atonement by repenting of our sins, being baptized, receiving the gift of the Holy Ghost, and obeying all of the commandments. In this way we are cleansed from sin."[17] Active Mormons do not view salvation as traditional Christians do, accomplished once and for all by Christ's death on the cross. Traditional Christians have only to receive this gift of Jesus, his death and resurrection, and follow the example and teachings of Jesus as revealed in the Bible. Because of the LDS belief that all mankind is saved (with the exception of those who accepted and then denied the truth

31

of the LDS gospel), the faithful Mormon aims for exaltation, with its attendant potential godhood—reaching the highest degree in the celestial kingdom (refer again to fig. 1). Exaltation *requires* obedience to the principles and ordinances of the LDS gospel.

The historical Christian church sees Eve's, and then Adam's, original sin as trying to usurp God's wisdom, *trying to become gods themselves.* This error brought death into the world and left humanity stuck in self-centeredness— the source of their (and our) sinfulness. Since God is not only a gracious God of justice but also a God of mercy, he sent Jesus to pay the ransom for our sins, and through believing in him, we disarm the consequences of the fall and are given eternal life. Other works are not *required* of us.

In my experience, the LDS church emphasizes neither sin nor grace, in general. In the 368 pages of *Gospel Principles,* only two pages are devoted to sin. While Mormons acknowledge Christ died for our sins, they speak more about his atoning sacrifice overcoming spiritual death. From the Mormon point of view, to sin is to open up the possibility of not being forgiven and the necessity of positive action by the sinner. According to Spencer W. Kimball in his definitive work, *The Miracle of Forgiveness,* "It depends upon whether or not you are forgiven, and when. It could be weeks, it could be years, it could be centuries before the happy day when you have the positive assurance that the Lord has forgiven you. That depends on your humility, your sincerity, your works, your attitudes."[18] This statement draws an even greater distinction between the LDS church and historical Christianity in terms of grace and forgiveness. Traditional Christians have the assurance of being forgiven immediately upon making a heartfelt request. The LDS church proposes something more than salvation and eternal life—exaltation (toward godhood) by works, which entails adherence to specified laws and ordinances. Traditional Christianity offers salvation by grace, the unearned gift of a loving God. In James R. White's *Letters to a Mormon Elder,* whom he calls Steve, he explains this distinction as a traditional Christian responding to LDS belief. He writes,

> What laws and ordinances are there in the free gospel of grace, Steve? Where are they? When I read about the Gospel in the New Testament, all I read about is the work of Jesus Christ and the sovereign grace of God. . . . I thank God daily that I do not have to stand before His aweful throne to be judged for my own righteousness. I will stand before Him with the righteousness of God in Christ Jesus (2 Cor. 5:17). I will not have to trust in a single meritorious action, a single act of obedience, because I know that no such thing can add to the work of Christ accomplished at Calvary.[19]

The most important difference between traditional Christianity and the LDS faith, however, is with authority and from whence it comes. In the evangelical church the Bible is authoritative. LDS doctrine maintains, however, that due to a total "apostasy" in the first century, the historic Christian church lost its authority.[20] Authority was then restored to Joseph Smith and is being conferred upon successive prophets. In the LDS church, authority stems from the word of the current prophet and subsequently ends in a "feeling" response of a receiver. (It must be noted, however, that personal confirmation or nonconfirmation does not supersede the validity of the prophecy.) "One of the pivotal doctrines of the Mormon religion is the belief in continuing revelation—that God 'will yet reveal many great and important things pertaining to the Kingdom of God.'"[21] Thus, many doctrinal tenets have come and gone: for example, the Adam/god doctrine, polygamy, and denial of ordination of African Americans to the priesthood, which is available to all Mormon boys at the age of twelve.

Additionally, the witness to the truth of the prophet's words lies in the experience of the hearer, because for most Mormons *feelings* are placed at the very core of religious truth. This is reflected in the passage in which God purportedly told Joseph Smith as he translated the Book of Mormon, "You must study it out in your mind; then you must ask me if it is right, and if it is right I will cause that your bosom will burn within you; therefore you shall feel that it is right" (*Doctrine and Covenants* 9:8). A feeling response, which Mormons believe to be guided by the Holy Ghost, is fundamental in LDS theology. From a traditional Christian point of view, this belief elevates emotions to unacceptable authority.

These different beliefs about the same words, the Godhead, grace and forgiveness, sin and authority frequently cause confusion between Mormons and traditional Christians. They also lead to misunderstandings that hinder Mormons struggling with needs unmet by their faith, or suffering from a loss of faith altogether, to find the direction, comfort, and peace traditional Christianity offers.

The next three chapters examine the issues that trouble the respondents I interviewed—both those who have left the church and those who still identify themselves as Mormons—and describe the patterns that emerged from their responses.

2
Needs Unmet by Mormonism

Many of the people I interviewed first doubted the LDS church because it failed to meet their basic needs. This is not for want of effort on the part of the church, for the LDS church honestly attempts to meet all its members' needs. According to former Mormon and author Janis Hutchinson, the church offers "classes in world cultures, music, homemaking, scouting, parenthood, service projects, morality, work ethics, speech, literature, drama, self-improvement, goal-setting—all effectively designed for the spiritual, physical, moral, intellectual, and emotional growth of its members."[1] For many members, however, the effort fails.

The LDS church also has a history and dogma that must be accepted. The church began with the visions of a young prophet who was led by heavenly visitors to golden plates buried in New York, which he translated through the divine assistance of "seer stones." The plates themselves are the text of the Book of Mormon, the word of God, a history of descendants of Abraham in the New World. This is the foundation of the church and also the grounds for questioning among the more discerning members.

To doubt any of this construct—the visits of the heavenly personages, the existence of the plates, the nature of the translating, and the validity of the text itself—casts doubt on all of it: the status of Joseph Smith as prophet and the truth of the scriptures, doctrine, and practices of the church. Joseph Smith is either a prophet or a charlatan; the scriptures are either the divine word of God or the inventions of an imposter.

Members *do* get the impression that they must take it all or leave it all. If they hold this absolute position, a doubt in any one area can often cause a complete meltdown in all areas—rejection of all beliefs. This absolutism combined with the authoritarian nature of church doctrine and structure compounds the pressure on the members. The General Authorities of the LDS church are viewed by members as acting in God's stead, and when a member is called by an authority for a position of leadership, he or she assumes that the call is from God. Coupled with the belief that God doesn't make mistakes, a member can have a crisis of faith even when one Sunday school teacher or a speaker delivering a sermon at a meeting is found wanting.

At an editorial conference about this book, my brother (now a disfellowshiped member of the LDS church) shared this story:

> When I was twelve or thirteen, a speaker at sacrament meeting [worship service] was delivering a sermon about

36

apostasy. I got the impression from his sermon that apostates were anathema to God and would be rejected by God for the blessings of the afterlife. And from his description I also concluded that my parents, both inactive Mormons at that time, were themselves apostates. I was devastated. I felt that I was being forced to choose between my parents, whom I loved, and my religion. I believed that I was sent to church because I was supposed to believe what I was taught there. We were Mormons and believed in Mormonism. That message had always been consistent and compelling. So when I discovered that my parents must be apostates and I wouldn't see them in heaven, I was torn in half.

Fortunately, when I got home from church my mother saw how distressed I was and asked me what was wrong. When I told her, she simply said, "You don't have to believe everything you hear at church." At that moment, irrevocably, my choice was made. I chose loyalty to my parents over loyalty to the church. I didn't clearly see it at the time, but I can see now that I simply ceased belief. At that moment I became merely a social Mormon.

For many other former Mormons, a single crack—a conflict of interpretation, an unmet need, a nagging doubt—can lead to crisis. While in my research I did not ask a question about needs unmet by the LDS church, as I went over the transcribed interviews, I noticed patterns. Many people just spontaneously shared their unmet needs as the foundation of their questioning the LDS faith.

My intention in quoting from these interviews is neither to confirm nor agree with the observations of the respondents but to record and describe their experiences in a context that can make their transition from the LDS church understandable.

Intellectual Needs

Freedom to Ask Questions

> Tim Schmall is an intense and dedicated thirty-one-year-old. He was raised in Provo, Utah, and was a truth-seeking Mormon for nineteen or twenty years. He is married and has two young boys.
>
> Tim describes himself as an armchair theologian. He volunteers one day a week at a Christian bookstore in Provo, where he is surrounded by the writings of the Christian masters. I met Tim in a New Testament Greek class in which he excelled. Tim has expressed a desire to do missionary work.

Tim Schmall had a natural sense of the one and only sovereign God. He recalls being told when he was twelve or younger "that the God whom [they] had, according to LDS theology, is one of many gods." Tim wrestled with this concept, then asked, "Who's the number one God?" The answer he recalls receiving was, "We don't know, so we don't ask," or "There isn't a number one, and if there is, it doesn't matter. We don't have anything to do with him." Tim remembers being "really distraught and disappointed about it." He recalls "going home and being afraid and upset and getting down on my knees to pray, sneaking a prayer: 'This prayer is to the number one God. I wish you could be my God.'"

Lynda Cooley, a master's level public school teacher who left active participation in the LDS church by the age of thirteen, had problems with unanswered questions. In spite of doctrinal admonitions to the contrary, Mormon culture expects "blind faith" of its members. Since women are ineligible for positions of authority (only men hold the priesthood, the source of LDS authority), they, in particular, are not encouraged to ask questions. This leaves bright women with many unanswered questions. As Lynda commented,

"I can't remember exactly when it started, but it was pretty early. If I asked too many questions, they would reprimand me for it."

Christine Campbell, a Ph.D. psychologist, noted, "I was afraid to ask questions." Brittany Fyans, a bright woman twenty years Christine's junior, was not afraid to ask, but received the admonition that "I would be condemned for not having faith—not having blind faith."[2] Both are struggling to make a rather recent adjustment to new churches.

But it was not just women who were admonished against questioning doctrine. Bryan Ohlsen, the former president of his high school debate team, was left with his intellectual curiosity unsatisfied. He said, "I had lists of question after question that I asked to people in authority." He was very disappointed with the responses he got of the "Well, that just wasn't for man to know" genre.

Ross Anderson, currently an Evangelical Free pastor, who questioned the LDS church when he lived in California, observed what happened when he tried to convert a traditional Christian girlfriend to the LDS church. They met with local LDS missionaries. "My girlfriend had answers to all the missionaries' questions. They didn't have answers to all hers." Ross was unsatisfied because his church did not have the best and final answer to all theological questions.

Resolving Historical Inconsistencies

Russ Lane is a thirty-seven-year-old Mormon history buff. He has lived and conducted research in Utah and the Midwestern site of the home of the Reorganized Latter-day Saint church. He has also lived in California. He is unmarried.

His love of history led him not only to research the Mormon archives and other early documents but also to speak publicly about what he found. He was excommunicated from the LDS church six years ago in California.

Music plays a big part in Russ's life and in his love of things religious. An organ player led him to his current church, which he attended for several years before accepting baptism.

Russ needed to resolve historical issues.

Russ Lane had lived in Iowa and was familiar with the practices of the Reorganized LDS church (RLDS). He tried to reconcile the differences between the LDS and Reorganized LDS doctrines because both churches were based on the same original scriptures. This put him on the path of historical investigation. He followed this intellectual quest upon his return to Salt Lake City. He took courses at the LDS Institute of Religion (theological training centers near universities and colleges in areas with a large concentration of Mormons) and eventually found himself doing research in the LDS church historian's office. As he said, "The historical thing was very interesting for me. That's what I focused on." In the end, he could not reconcile the deception by a con man, Mark Hoffman, who had sold fake documents to church authorities.[3] "If they [church authorities] are truly inspired, how come they aren't open to the inspiration to know that these were deceptions?" His lament was, "They spent my tithing money buying these documents."

At the time of the Mark Hoffman events, University of Utah philosophy professor Sterling M. McMurrin, a faithful Mormon on his own terms, said, "We are going through a stage of indoctrination in the church that robs the individual of intellectual freedom." He continued, "To a remarkable degree the church has concealed much of its history from its people, while at the same time causing them to tie their religious faith to its own controlled interpretation of its history." With alarm and amazement, McMurrin contended that church leaders such as Boyd K. Packer "regard genuine honest church history as dangerous to the faith."[4]

> Richard (pseudonym) is a businessman in his late forties who is not a native of Salt Lake. He was raised in the LDS mission field in California and the Midwest.
>
> His leadership roles in the LDS church began when he was president of his deacons quorum. He says, "I was in bishoprics and stake [one level above the ward] high councils before I had even turned thirty, married in the temple, went to BYU, pretty orthodox." He attained an advanced degree from the University of Utah.
>
> Richard's study to strengthen his knowledge about and belief in the LDS gospel led to his becoming a "reform-minded" member. He "has spent the last twenty years involved in LDS periodical publishing, both editing and writing, and also in a variety of independent periodical and book publishing companies."
>
> He and his wife are now separated. Richard describes himself as a secular humanist.

Richard, too, had problems reconciling the Mormon history. As he said, "I was a debater all through school. I had intellectual friends who were not Mormon. . . . I came to determine that the church was not what it had represented itself to be in categories like its history, its manipulation of its history, its rewriting of its history."

Spiritual Needs

Alan, who asked to be identified by first name only, professes to be a committed, albeit nonattending, Mormon. He began attending a Sunday night religious service held by a group of questioning or reform-minded Mormons when church sponsored activities failed to meet his needs. As he said, "I was always hungry for spiritual involvement or contact that I didn't feel like I was getting necessarily in the church involvement I had. . . . Maybe it was because there wasn't enough time to develop a conversation in a Sunday school class. You didn't feel as free to talk about things really personal, or there may have been an element of fear that trespassing on someone else's perceptions wasn't appropriate."

Among Mormons, a Scripture frequently cited is, "Be ye therefore perfect, even as your Father which is in heaven is perfect" (Matt. 5:48 KJV). In the minds of many Mormons, this admonition allows no room for error. Two former Mormon women spoke of carrying the burden of living in a legalistic culture. Tawna Robinson said that she didn't begin questioning the church until after she had received the Lord. "I never questioned the church but my ability to live up to the rules. What I was seeking was a relationship with God. I just kept trying to do the rules as best I could, and I remember being very depressed and trying harder."

Brittany Fyans, too, struggled with her imperfection at keeping the commandments. She struggled to gain a testimony of the truth of the LDS gospel. "I had to live a perfect, perfect life. If my mind would wander at all in church, I would pray for forgiveness. I did it all—and I didn't have a testimony. I knew there was a God, but I didn't have this burning in the bosom."

Pastor Ross, too, doubted himself and not the LDS church. His older brother was on a mission in a very primitive area. He, of course, was expected to go on a mission two years hence, and he wondered to himself, "Do I have a strong enough conviction and believe this enough to go into those circumstances?" He felt that his security in the LDS church was threatened by his asking that question. This is understandable in the light of the "all or nothing" way that the church is viewed by many members.

Emotional Needs

The respondents also discussed emotional needs that were not acknowledged in or by the church. Niki Payne, a convert to the LDS church in her teens, spoke about her internal journey away from the LDS church: It "began with disillusionment about the goodness of the church. I began to struggle with depression in about 1975. The church didn't seem to accommodate my needs, nor did it respond to my needs."

Psychologist Christine Campbell, for example, could only refer to feelings of discomfort, "just not feeling good." All she knew was that she started feeling uncomfortable in church when she was in high school. Nevertheless, she went to college at Brigham Young University, but she found the new freedom of being away from her parents gave her an opportunity to skip church. She found that she "felt better not going than going." Because the Mormon church uses the language of feeling, there is always an expectation that "feeling" needs will be met, and it can be a shock when they are not.

> Cindy Lou Blackmon is a thirty-four-year-old mother of three who is now remarried to a Christian engineer/theology student.
>
> She was a Mormon "star" until she found out that she was a second-class Mormon, being required to do what her then husband said. The conflicts they were having led her to leave the marriage, the church, and the culture.
>
> Cindy is not afraid to take strong stands both in her life and her religion.

Cindy Lou Blackmon spoke about having needs met and then having that fulfillment withdrawn. She got her self-esteem by being a "star" in the church, knowing the Book of Mormon inside and out, witnessing to every non-Mormon she met, bearing a moving and powerful testimony. On the first Sunday of every month, the Mormon sacrament meeting (worship service) is designated a testimony meeting. Members are invited to proclaim their belief in Joseph Smith, the current prophet, the Book of Mormon, and whatever other personal witness might be "felt" appropriate. This is called "bearing your testimony." It is a good opportunity to train the young, who are coached to repeat the words of their parents, "I believe that Joseph Smith was a true prophet of God. . . ." When she began to have problems in her marriage and asked to meet with the bishop (a lay pastor equivalent, called to serve for five to six years), she got a surprise. She discovered she was a second-class Mormon because she was not a male. (All authority in the LDS church is passed down through a chain of a male hierarchy. Only men hold the priesthood. Women gain their place in the eternal progression through their marriage to a man.) The bishop spoke about her husband: "He has a special anointing from God and you have to listen to him." Cindy Lou was devastated. "I began to hate the arrogance I thought I saw in most Mormon men."

The Need to Trust

Will McGarvey, currently a Presbyterian youth minister, mentioned having his security threatened by what he perceived as problems with the "divine inspiration" of the authorities of the church. His mission call, a supposedly divinely inspired call issued by a letter from the LDS church president, was originally for Jamaica. He "couldn't get a visa to go there," and he was recalled to Maine. This caused his first doubts of the inspiration by God of the church authorities.

The Need to Belong

The parents of my cousin Alyce Covey seldom attended church services. Though not a member of the church, her father cooked special dinners for the congregation. Alyce reported a humiliating incident when she was about ten or eleven. "In a Sunday school class, when one of the [teacher's hypothetical] questions was, 'You are going to have house guests. They are used to having coffee for breakfast. Are you going to serve it? Those of you who would serve it, raise your hand.' I happily raised my hand and looked around and no one else had raised their hand." Alyce reported being humiliated. And what made the humiliation worse was that she was then verbally demeaned by the teacher for the choice she had made.

Always the seeker, Karen Clark's doubts were kindled a little earlier, at the time of her baptism, but they were not initially recognized as doubts about the church. They were doubts about herself. In the weekday classes held for children of grammar school age, her teacher had said, "If you [are] very holy and very special, it [is] not uncommon to see an angel inside the room" in which the baptism took place. Karen was deeply disappointed when she did not see that angel as she came out of the water.

As she reported, "I kept wondering what happened, why I didn't feel special or anything. I thought something was just very, very dysfunctional with me because it didn't take. . . . I wanted to discover what was missing in both me and the church. . . . Why don't I fit? Maybe I don't believe strongly enough. Maybe I'm not praying right." This kind of thinking is a heavy burden for a child of eight.

The Consequences of Unmet Needs

These events described by the respondents may appear inconsequential out of context. We all have unmet needs; we all suffer humiliations in childhood. But for a member of an organization that claims to be the sole agent of God's

45

truth and complete answer to its members' needs, an otherwise small event can have life-changing consequences.

During our interview, I talked with Karen about the three categories of unmet needs I had observed—intellectual, emotional, and spiritual. She suggested that if a person is wounded in one area, he or she will look to the other areas for healing. If in that search further wounding occurs, it sets a person up to leave the church and seek healing elsewhere.

In the next chapter, I record the respondents' continuing process of investigation, their search for healing, and their failure to find it. First, however, I need to include Wayne's experience. He is an exception to the usual process of discovering unmet needs in the process of leaving the LDS church.

> Wayne (pseudonym) is a sixty-seven-year-old retired university professor and musician, active in music circles in his community. He has eight children, six of whom have completed LDS missions. He reports a sudden conversion out of Mormonism at the age of forty-five. He had done no serious questioning prior to that point.
>
> While answering questions honestly, Wayne is circumspect about having left the Mormon church. He still attends, occasionally, to please his wife. He reported that he had heard that his former stake president had issued an order that he "was not to have a forum at the church," meaning he could not teach a class or speak at meetings.

As Wayne reported: "I had no dissatisfaction at all with my life in the church. Everything was going along beautifully. At the age of forty-five I had eight children, a good profession, and was a member of the general board of Mutual Improvement Association, an LDS church youth auxiliary. I found the association and work totally delightful in every respect. I had no reason whatever to want to change anything. Our family life was church centered."

Wayne went on to describe the circumstances surrounding his "conversion" event: "It really goes back to the Mormon idea that church members should seek revelatory experiences to confirm this or that aspect of their spiritual life. . . . In a susceptible moment of grace perhaps, I made a commitment that I would act upon what I perceived to be the whisperings of the Holy Ghost and I would accept the consequences. In the next moment, everything had changed. I shed very quickly most of what had been my Mormon costume. . . . Overnight, the church lost its power over me."

This loss was, using Karen's metaphor, Wayne's spiritual wound. It led him on a search to heal that wound through "intense religious practice, mostly reading, meditation and stuff like that." He reported that it took several months before he "had the courage to share this" life-changing experience with anybody.

Wayne obviously did not move from a sense of unmet needs. But most of the respondents quoted in this chapter responded to a keen sense of need—intellectual, spiritual, or emotional—that led them toward action.

3

Motivations
to Question Further

After their initial doubts, the respondents questioned the LDS church further. There is great diversity in these stories, but for the sake of organization, I categorize the respondents' motivations to question the church as spiritual, emotional, and intellectual. Some respondents have complex motivations, and some have simple.

Their dissatisfaction with the LDS church led most of the respondents to ask specific questions, either in trying to get their needs met or in seeking an explanation as to why their needs were not met. Human beings respond in three ways to a perceived problem: (1) there's something wrong with me, (2) there's something wrong with them (other people), or (3) there's something wrong with it (the situation). Among those interviewed, the ones who experienced the most pain were the ones who had to move from "there's something wrong with me" to "there's something wrong with the LDS church." But grace carried them on in their quest for a solution to their problems.

Intellectual Questions

Sandra Tanner is a fifty-three-year-old who has committed her life to being an information resource to former Mormons and those investigating leaving the LDS church. With her husband, Jerald, she has produced reproductions of many early Mormon documents. Her Lighthouse Ministry runs a small bookstore that is a delight to visit for the latest books on the LDS church and some conversation.

Sandra, a direct descendent of Brigham Young, was convinced to leave the LDS church after she met Jerald, a questioning Mormon. Sandra simultaneously was converted to follow the biblical Jesus. Yet she held on to the truth of the Book of Mormon for about three years after her conversion.

Sandra is a well-known author and lecturer.

For Sandra Tanner, a boyfriend who was questioning the LDS church motivated her to do the same. "When Jerald started showing me that there were early Mormon documents and comparing them to the current ones, seeing how everything had been changed—doctrines changed and scriptures changed—those became major problem areas." This discovery of the mutability of the LDS church doctrine led Sandra eventually to leave and to investigate traditional Christianity. Jerald and Sandra later married and went on to become internationally renowned resources on the LDS church, particularly on early Mormon documents.

Evah Bigler was a beneficiary of the Tanners' research. Her questions began as soon as she left Utah for the first time, "seeing how others viewed Mormons." That experience led her to study church history.

The Tanners also influenced the history buff, Russ Lane, who said of his experience in Iowa with the Reorganized LDS church, "I was always open-minded, because we had the truth, so it didn't bother me." Russ had a real historical thirst. Then he was introduced to the Tanners' research, which "came highly recommended to me by an Institute teacher [with these words], 'Their research is always accurate and always with integrity.' They reproduce a lot of things I'm interested in as a historian." This thirst for historical knowledge led him eventually to leave the church.

Tim Schmall, the respondent who wanted to know the "number one God," had many seeds of doubt sown early on. He vacillated between periods of using illegal drugs and practicing other non-Mormon behaviors and periods of being a committed Mormon brother (male member). His confusion regarding the truth of the LDS gospel crested in the U.S. Marine Corps. A confrontation with a marine junior drill instructor led him to investigate the LDS church. As he tells it, "'So, it says here that you're a Mormon. What the hell kind of religion is that?' I blanked. 'Sir, the private doesn't know, sir.' . . . That's when I began to wake up. I didn't know what I professed to believe."

Alan, however, possibly thought too much about his beliefs. "I don't know what it means to be intellectually satisfied," said Alan. He was explaining his unhappiness regarding the rumors that circulated about his reasons for leaving the LDS church, speculation that he had "thought" himself out of the church. He said, "I am intellectually committed to the church, and, in fact, the thing that keeps me involved and committed and in wonder about my faith is the passion to know about it. That is the greatest attraction of Mormonism as I understand it."

Mormons in Transition

But Alan is a contradiction. Later he added, "I would say I haven't left. . . . I don't follow the rules. I don't practice the orthodoxies. I don't do conventional things that are associated with Mormonism."

At the age of twelve, upon returning from two years in Europe with her family, Karen Clark (who had been disappointed in not seeing angels after her baptism) began to perceive a big difference in the LDS church compared to other churches. In Germany she had been attending an American community church where "everything I said was interesting. I could talk to my assistant pastor, and he was really interested. Everything I thought was interesting. If I said something he would say, 'Well, did you think of this?' or 'Did you think of that? That's really a good thought. Let me show you where that shows up in the Bible.' My thoughts were already in the Bible! . . . That really turned things around for me, the beginning of questioning [the LDS church]."

When Karen returned home, she became another victim of unanswered questions. As she said, "I was trained to ask questions, and the questions were not satisfied. [When I'd ask] a question that required an astute philosophical answer, I was invited to stand in the hall."

Spiritual Questions

Will McGarvey is an intense twenty-seven-year-old who is dedicated to bringing traditional Christianity to the youth in Salt Lake City. He began to question the LDS church on his mission for it and then came to historical Christianity. His wife has made a similar decision since the time of our interview.

Will started H.I.S.[1] clubs for Christian youth, which are designed to compete with the LDS seminary classes in Salt Lake high schools, for which schools release students from class to

52

attend. He has been appointed youth minister at a large Presbyterian church, also since our interview.

Will is very knowledgeable about the differences between LDS church doctrine and historical Christianity.

Will McGarvey spoke of his life after completing his mission. "Within a year, standing on my own power, I couldn't keep the commandments." He had "made promises that I couldn't live up to." He said of that time, "I felt pretty guilty. It made me look twice at the source of those [commandments]. . . . I wanted to make sure that these things were true."

Tawna Robinson felt guilty about her inability to live up to LDS church rules. "I just carried around more and more guilt. When I was going to college, I decided to go to LDS dorms, to be around spiritual people. We were paired with boys who were returned missionaries. . . . I went out with two of them, and I have never been so brutally attacked, sexually attacked [physically] as with those two. They were much worse than I had ever encountered. Here I thought I was with super-spiritual people. . . . After that quarter, I went to the regular dorms. I gave up. There's no way I can be perfect. There's no way I can win God's approval." This surrender actually opened her to representatives of Campus Crusade (a Christian evangelical organization active on college campuses) the next year.

Brittany Fyans, who was rebuffed for asking questions, went to BYU for a year and left feeling unfulfilled and guilty, "feeling like I wasn't complete. . . . I tried to see the world through God's eyes. . . . [I] felt like the Mormon church thought it was evil to try to understand God. . . . I want to know the God I'm worshiping. I broke free . . . started looking at other cultures." This interest in other ways of life led her to investigate traditional Christianity.

Former debate team president Bryan Ohlsen questioned the issues of repentance and forgiveness. "As a Mormon it's impossible to be truly forgiven for anything. If you repent and then do it again, it's like you had never repented in the first place. I had a couple of things like that, that I really didn't want to tell my bishop. I didn't think they were any of his business, and I figured that, as a man, he didn't have any place to forgive me for them in the first place. For that reason, I was having turmoil for a couple of years." During this period Bryan met a Christian with whom he could speak honestly about LDS and Christian doctrines.

Emotional Questions

After having been divorced for over five years from what was supposed to be an eternal temple marriage, the disappointed Lena, who asked to be anonymous, was dating her first boyfriend. She was preparing to move her family to a new home, and as she described it, "I had been a little bit sexual with a man [but] not intercourse or anything. I went to talk to my former bishop before I moved, and he said, 'It's not my business. Talk to your new bishop.' I was not willing to talk to a strange man. I was furious that *my* bishop would tell me to talk to a strange man about something like having my clothes off with another man. It was none of his business. I didn't go back to church." This incident shows little understanding on the part of Lena's bishop of the trust that develops between confidantes.

Christine Campbell, a psychologist who could only express her questioning of the LDS church through her feelings of discomfort, spoke about her depression. "If I didn't accept the LDS church, I was going to hell anyway, so it didn't make much difference." Try as she might, she still believed that she was doomed to spend eternity in hell for not making it.

54

> Niki Payne is a forty-four-year-old mother of four teenage children. She converted to the LDS church from the Baptist church. She had been writing to a boy on a mission (whom she later married), which may have influenced her decision. She became convinced that Mormonism was a divinely inspired restoration of the original gospel, which allowed her to tolerate a lot of doctrinal discrepancies. She held to that conviction until deep and ongoing depression led her back to the Bible.
>
> She lost her marriage to her missionary pen pal through her decision to leave Mormonism. She does have custody of her four Mormon children. She and the kids are still trying to build healthy relationships of trust given their religious differences.

Niki Payne, who converted to the LDS church at eighteen years of age, talked about the depression that ultimately led her to question the LDS church: "In 1988 [at the age of thirty-eight], I began to see a therapist for my recurring and ongoing depression. Therapy helped me identify my belief that only God would lead me to wellness and that only God was truly faithful and trustworthy. I began to study the Bible. I began to seek other ways of relating to God."

Cultural Mormons

These are the kinds of experiences—intellectual, spiritual, and emotional—that led the seekers to question the LDS church and to look for answers outside the church. They are examples only. They are typical only in the most general sense: These people had questions for which the church's doctrine, practices, or history provided insufficient responses. Many people who leave the LDS church, however, are the sort of people who will take action when dissatisfied and will seek a solution to discomfort. Of those I interviewed, however, Larry DuBois fits a category of his own.

Larry DuBois is a fifty-two-year-old businessman and writer. He attended the LDS church for his first fifteen or sixteen years. After that he has only attended occasional funerals of friends and family members.

Larry's family hails from Idaho, though Larry grew up in Salt Lake City. He left Utah after high school and has lived in New York, Washington, D.C., Chicago, Miami, and Los Angeles. Larry says he has been proud of his Mormon heritage and pleased to admit to being a Mormon. Larry was at first unwilling to give his full name.

As Larry DuBois explained, "I went to the Mormon church as a little boy because my mother made me. I went to Sunday school and priesthood meetings—deacons, teachers, priests. I was a deacon and passed the sacrament [the LDS equivalent of communion], but the reason was that I had a key to the church gymnasium. I played basketball, and I didn't want to lose that key." Larry explains that when he was in high school and had access to the high school's gymnasium, he "gave the key to the gymnasium back. And I've never set foot in the church again, except for an occasional funeral."

And yet, Larry considers himself a Mormon. "I still regard myself as a Mormon. . . . I have Mormon blood in me. My ancestor was very close to Joseph Smith and very close to Brigham Young. He performed some of Joseph Smith's marriages. . . . And so nobody can tell me that I'm not a Mormon. My Mormon blood is as good and strong and sound as anybody who lives in this valley today." He reiterated, "In terms of lineage, background, I still regard myself as a Mormon." Larry is what is described as a cultural Mormon—one who has ceased belief and practice but still identifies himself as and frequently has the societal values of a Mormon.

Some of the respondents questioned the LDS church because of historical inaccuracies. One has replaced his LDS belief system yet holds on to church by a thread. For others the inability to keep the commandments perfectly led them to question. Still others just gave up in their sinfulness. Larry remains a Mormon in identification alone, but for most of the respondents, their sense of unmet needs and their investigation led them to particular criticisms of the LDS church, its doctrine, or its practices.

4
Criticism from within the LDS Church

Of the twenty-five people I interviewed, only the ones who identified themselves as Mormons were critical of the LDS church. I heard only one of the former Mormons I interviewed say anything negative about the LDS church. At first, I assumed the former Mormons were at peace with the church, but that supposition is open to conjecture. I didn't ask either group specifically to critique or judge the LDS church.

This behavior reminds me of how we behave in a bad marriage or other intimate relationship. We are critical of the other person when we are dependent on or enmeshed with them. When we free ourselves of dependence and know who we are independently, we no longer need to be critical. And so it appears to be the case with Mormons in transition and their dependence on the church.

Authoritarianism

As Wayne, who was "converted" out of Mormonism, pointed out, "I guess that my biggest surprise is that members allow the church so much power. It's very simple to say no and to not be dependent on what the church says about a particular thing. I'm certainly grateful when the church doesn't take a stand on something, [when people ask], 'What is the church's stand on this or that?' . . . The fewer stands the church takes, the more freedom individuals have to make up their own minds."

But by the very nature of the LDS church, as with all authoritarian religions where a human being is the ultimate authority rather than Scripture or the biblical Jesus Christ, there are opportunities for abuse. Authority figures can depend on this authority to gain power and control. This was one area in which the respondents criticized the LDS church.

Karen Clark is a fifty-four-year-old divorced mother of two grown daughters. As a child she experienced the isolation that comes from having a university professor for a father and living within a predominantly working-class ward (local congregation). She also attended a private school on the university campus, which increased her isolation in the neighborhood.

Karen has always struggled with belonging in the LDS church. This led her to a wide variety of spiritual alternatives, including two attempts to return to the LDS church as an adult.

I met Karen in high school and we became close friends. We spent most of the next thirty years living in different states but have always maintained that initial bond.

Karen Clark, who looked for angels at her baptism, was hurt by the authoritarian nature of the LDS church when she went to a private school and was not allowed to attend church activities with her friends. At that time, weekday education classes (primary) were held after school. To get to primary in her neighborhood ward, she had to walk two miles on Wednesday, and she always arrived late. This made her an outcast with her peers in her church. She begged her family and local church authorities to let her go to a different ward for primary, one closer to her school, but her requests were denied. "So I was forced to go to a ward where I knew no one."

Larry DuBois admitted having a visceral reaction to organized religion and said that it comes "straight from my feelings toward the authorities in the LDS church. These guys are about money, property, and prestige. They are about power and control. They are about authoritarianism. They are about narrow-mindedness. They are about better than thou, holier than thou. They are not about the spiritual principles that have come down through the ages."

Alyce Covey described the authoritarian nature of the church as "the least appealing part of the church—the punishing. I know that's a way you keep people in line. . . . [But] why keep people in line? Because it's partly a business." While aware of its authoritarian nature, Alyce graciously accepts the church and its foibles. In fact, Alyce defends the church "when people are highly critical. It's definitely part of what I'm about." She listed the things she honors in the church and what it has done in Utah: "The value of [the] family, the value of [personal] industry, the value of maintaining property for others to appreciate. Succeeding, [the] positive side of competition. . . . I've had the pleasure of absolutely choosing what I liked and leaving the rest."

61

Rules

The LDS church is a legalistic church, one that requires obedience to certain ordinances and principles for full membership. For many members, obedience is difficult. Alan, who loves and is committed to the church, commented on how difficult it is for him to keep the required commandments: "If we were good people, living a set of rules . . . then we're worthy. We get the ticket to go to the temple. I've never been able to do that [keep the rules], ever, ever, ever. . . . There are so many things to be guilty about, even the little rules."

In *The Subtle Power of Spiritual Abuse,* the authors list three reasons traditional Christians believe God gave the law (or rules). "First, He gave the Law so that we could see that we have sinned. God's standard is like a mirror that shows us our performance has fallen short of God's expectation [Rom. 3:20]. . . .

"The second purpose of the Law is to convince us that we are helpless, through our own efforts, to hit the mark [Rom. 11:32]. . . . God's Law was not given as a means to peace with God. Neither is it to challenge us to live holy lives. It was given to show us that peace with God and holy lives are absolutely unattainable through self-effort. God's Law imprisons and defines us as persons who are in a state of missing the mark.

"The third purpose of the Law is to bring us into a *grace-full* relationship with God on the basis of His own work of grace through Christ [Rom. 11:32]. . . . God offers peace and right standing with Himself as a gift at His own expense."[1]

But it appears that for Alan, as well as for other questioning Mormons, there is little understanding as to why God gave the law. Many Mormons see the commandments of the church as arbitrary and man-made rather than divine in origin.

Domination

Larry DuBois, who left the LDS church when he acquired his high school gym key, admitted he is angry and expressed this anger toward the LDS church freely: "That church is about corporate domination. That's frankly all they care about, the guys who run the church. Privately, you know, maybe some of them are nice guys, privately maybe some of them try to make the church do better, and privately maybe some of them care about members of the church. But behind them are ruthless, power-hungry men."

We must note that payment of a 10 percent tithe is a requirement for receiving a recommendation to go to the temple. Members meet with their bishop at year's end for tithing reconciliation.

I, too, felt the weight of the church's domination. It seemed as though we weren't allowed to think for ourselves. We were supposed to follow the party line.

One True Church

Richard, who identified himself as both a Mormon and a secular humanist, addressed the LDS church's claim to be the one true church. There is no such thing. "There isn't one and only one true IBM or government! Organizations aren't true. Maybe there's a belief or a concept that is true. But there is not an exclusive system of truth, whether it's religious or humanistic or political or whatever."

Lena, the one who felt betrayed by her bishop when she confessed to him her sexual activity,[2] had strong reactions to this concept: "My basic objection to the Mormon church is that they say they are the only church that has all the truth, that some other churches have some of the truth, but that *they* have it all. I see that statement as a divisive kind of thing . . . setting up an 'us' and 'them'—a schism. And that scares me."

Abusive churches often claim to be the one and only true church or to have some special knowledge that other churches do not have. In *Churches That Abuse,* Ronald Enroth states, "Followers are led to think that there is no other church quite like theirs and that God has singled them out for special purposes. Other, more traditional, evangelical churches are put down. Subjective experience is emphasized and dissent is discouraged. . . . Rules and legalism abound. People who don't follow the rules or who threaten exposure are often dealt with harshly. Excommunication is common. For those who leave, the road back to normalcy is difficult."[3] This description matches my experience and that of several of those interviewed of the difficult process of leaving the LDS church.

Divine Guidance

In reviewing his experience in the church, Richard said, "I also came to question the decisions—the policies—of the leaders. I [saw them] providing revelation [in which it was] very difficult to see the hand of God. I could see the hand of men—fallible men—making decisions, good, bad, and indifferent. I saw the same traits that you'd see in any big organization, that is, the tendency to value conformity over individuality and creativity of expression—the tendency to support the purposes of the institution against the purposes of the individual."

Richard, who sat on a stake high council and on an excommunication board before his belief decayed into nonbelief, went on to list the reasons for this switch: "Church politics, history, claims to divine guidance, its requirement [for] absolute obedience . . . its persecution of those who are intellectuals—those who would improve the church—

the absolute unwillingness to learn anything from its own members and listen to them. All of these things are combined to cause me not to believe in the basic truth of the claims of Mormonism."

Narrowness

In reflecting on her process of leaving the church, including several attempts to return, Karen Clark described the narrowness of the thinking of those in leadership positions in the LDS church. A Sunday school teacher emotionally devastated Karen's artistic daughter when the teacher told the class that a very simple Thanksgiving turkey was all the children should be able to draw at that age. The girl was already doing much more than hand-tracing turkeys. Karen was also told she would need a letter from her nonbelieving husband giving his permission before Karen could attend services. "That's totally it. They all had the same kind of thinking. There was this little box, whether it was about art or about having my husband sign a letter, whether it was about my being kicked out of class because I thought for myself. I finally got the picture. I said, 'I can't do it, anymore!'"

Richard objected to the narrowness with an analogy to basketball: "People who were proud of their narrowness, people who were critical of thinkers [were] like a bad referee in a basketball game, who will just keep calling fouls, unrighteously, just to get even. I've seen that kind of pettiness go on."

Excommunication

The church excommunicated Larry DuBois's cousin, an event that caused Larry a lot of pain: "I saw the emotional devastation that it wreaked on him, and I thought the church isn't supposed to be about wreaking emotional devastation on people. The church is supposed to be about helping people. . . . A lifetime of experiences like that left me alienated from . . . the institution of the Mormon church."

> Alyce Covey is my cousin. She lived in Salt Lake City while I was living in the Los Angeles area. I was surprised, during one of my returns to the LDS church in 1988, to find that she played piano every Sunday for the primary, the grammar school children's education arm.
>
> Alyce has a very pragmatic view of Mormonism, one she has held since childhood. She has what she calls a God-given gift, her piano playing ability, and so feels it is appropriate to share this gift with the church.
>
> Alyce is married and is very active in civic and philanthropic affairs in Salt Lake City.

Alyce Covey, with her gentle heart, commented on excommunication: "I think that I would imagine if I were running a church, it would be more important to bring people in and spend more time with them instead of casting them out." Alyce has the ability to overlook slights and insults. She has a forgiving heart. She acknowledged having found no perfect system, either in her family or in organizations.

Larry spoke about what he found when he returned to Salt Lake City in 1992: "I started paying attention to some of the controversies that had been going on here in the past few years, the people who have been excommunicated—men and women alike—because they haven't been standing up for the church line. [People were] trying to have a sane, intelligent dialogue about church authority. And the church's response was to excommunicate them. Apparently a lot of people are unhappy about that."

Alan, however, admitted to abusing the Mormon church's minor disciplinary measures with a response appropriate to a rules-dominated structure. "The church's disciplinary process has led me to abusing it. 'Well, I've done that, now I can sin some more,' instead of honestly wanting to live this kind of life."

The Role of Women

The role of women in the LDS church drew some criticism from the people interviewed. For example, Lena said, "I object to women not holding the priesthood in their own right, [instead of] through the men. I object [that there aren't] women bishops, [that women] aren't able to give blessings—the laying on of hands. I would like to see them giving the sacrament. I would like to see a woman prophet."

Alyce Covey's comment was, "I just think they're afraid of us." But, as usual, Larry DuBois had a much more visceral reaction: "I still, when we sit here and talk about it, feel that visceral hostility. I felt anger at men putting themselves in positions of control over others. . . . I don't understand Mormon women who hook into that. Over the years I've run into women who were 'having trouble with the church.' My reaction has always been almost like Henny Youngman, 'Okay, so? Go away. Who cares?'"

But it's not that easy, of course, just to go away. There is a price to pay in this world and a threat of a price in the life hereafter. Larry continued, "Threat of outer darkness, if they leave. . . . They are doing spiritual abuse on people with that—on their own people!"

African Americans in the Priesthood

The decision to allow African Americans to hold the priesthood, which means allowing them to have a full membership in the LDS church, was made in 1978. Larry commented, "I watched from afar. . . . I think I was living in Washington, D.C., when someone was having a revelation—when the political pressure was getting large—a revelation that it was okay to let blacks into the priesthood. I remember being quite struck by the political timing of God's word to the church."

But as Richard pointed out, this political fluidity was nothing new: "They jettisoned polygamy, blood atonement, communitarianism, and some other things like Mother God before the turn of the century to gain statehood, avoid persecution, and to gain acceptance. . . . Then getting rid of the black prohibition, to me, was totally political. There's an example of a doctrine that was never scriptural, was never voted on by a congregation, that just became a doctrine by oral tradition. And it took a revelation to get rid of something that never was a doctrine in the first place."

History

As I mentioned earlier, Richard is critical of the church's handling of what he calls "the Mark Hoffman fiasco, where church leaders were buying documents, hiding them in the vault. [They were] trying to hide them from the members of the church, because they were afraid that the members couldn't handle the negative information. They didn't trust the members enough—looking at members in such a condescending way."

A couple other respondents mentioned their concerns about the church's history. Alyce Covey, at an age when she was trying to reconcile the Joseph Smith story, "had many Shriners in the neighborhood." What she was being taught at church didn't make sense to her, so the Shriners "would discuss that with me and tell me what he had taken from the [Masonic] temples. . . . I thought [Joseph Smith] was an extremely good marketing individual. I looked at him in terms of marketing. How do people market their ideas? Where do they go first to get the word out? . . . I just assumed he was clever with words and with people."

Larry DuBois mused on what "strain [existed] in the American character that this guy, Joseph Smith, created one of the world's greatest religions, if you define great by economic power, intellectual power, [and] control. . . . Somehow all this nonsense of his has left a very powerful legacy— miraculously enough by supposedly socially acceptable, educated, powerful people."

Psychotherapy

> I spoke to Lena (pseudonym) about this project after I heard her speak about still wearing her temple garments (special underwear that are to be worn after going through the LDS temple), even though she had been out of the LDS church for over five years.
>
> Since that time, Lena has been reintroduced to church attendance through a romantic interest. The romance has waned but her interest has continued. She admits to not knowing whether the outcome will be a return to faithfulness or a completion of her leaving.
>
> Lena is a divorced mother of two teenagers.

Lena was critical of the church's stand on the subject of psychotherapy: "It was not the church that saved me when my husband left. It was therapy. However, a close connection with God was necessary. . . . There were many people in my ward that were supportive. . . . But at this last conference (October 1995, a general semiannual conference of the church), 'Come to church and don't go to therapy' was the message. '[You can't] rely too much on psychologists.'" Lena exclaimed, "As if they served a competing function, even a similar function. To me, therapy and the church serve two different functions."

Image Alteration

For years, in the old visitor's center on the Salt Lake Mormon Temple grounds, a history of the church was presented. In that presentation, assertions were made that Mormonism was not a Christian religion, that it was the restoration of the true gospel of Jesus Christ. In recent times, however, the church has presented itself as a Christian denomination.

In our interview Richard said, "You have some Mormons . . . who are champions of neo-orthodox thinking being infused into Mormonism. They're trying to take this grace stuff and other ideas from Protestantism . . . and infuse it into Mormonism to give Mormonism a more Christian mainstream image, which they hope will be more appealing to potential converts. . . . I know that they [church authorities] do a lot of surveys. They closely monitor how they're perceived and where they find success and where they don't." Richard mentioned one of those surveys: "[The Mormon authorities] have done a study that shows that during the lifetime of an active Mormon, every active Mormon, 75 percent fall away for some period. But 68 percent come back and stay in." Richard observed that "the less active members, as they are now called, are the best candidates for [re]conversion by the [LDS] missionaries."[4]

In the light of Richard's comments about the LDS church's attempts to infuse mainstream Christianity into the church and its taking of surveys, Janis Hutchinson in *Out of the Cults and into the Church* says,

> I believe it [Mormonism] will survive, not because it had a divine origin or because God is necessarily sustaining it,

70

but because it has and will continue to exert strong control, promote fear in its membership—in other words, utilize all the necessary principles and strategies to successfully get through each stage it encounters. A movement will always prosper *without* God if it

- follows the necessary principles as established in the stages of all successful mass movements,
- changes structure and leadership at crucial points,
- meets the sociological needs of its general membership,
- maintains tight control,
- and makes periodic accommodations to society.[5]

Hutchinson goes on, "Accommodation is crucial for a movement to maintain itself if it wants to survive beyond the first or second generation."[6]

I spoke to Wayne, a prominent figure in Salt Lake who deconverted from the LDS church, about why he thinks he has not been called into an excommunication court. He responded, "I think you are correct in assuming that the church is probably reluctant to pursue public figures like [he named three well-known University of Utah faculty members]. I believe I have received preferential treatment in my ward because of my reputation. They're kind to me where they might not be to someone else. They really go overboard trying to make me feel welcome."

Good and Evil

Alan is a divorced father of two sons and a daughter. He is a former adjunct faculty member of the Brigham Young University Law School. Alan is also an admitted recovering alcoholic. He points to his alcoholism as the reason he stopped regularly attending the LDS church—having to end the duplicity of living two lives upon attaining sobriety. He now finds that the "LDS belief system is difficult to reconcile with" the personal powerlessness he believes he needs to acknowledge in order to maintain his sobriety.

Alan is faithful in his love for the LDS church. As we talked, it became apparent to me that he has discarded belief in (or as he calls it, "suspension of all judgment regarding") almost all the basic LDS doctrines. He holds on only to the church's fluidity—his interpretation for the doctrinal changes in the church: "the ongoing revelation. There's always more. It's going to be revealed one way or another, either institutionally or personally." Alan insists on his status as a Mormon.

At the time of our interview, Alan mused that "it would be easy for me to say that I was dissatisfied with the church institutionally, with all the smugness, and orthodoxies, and inflexibilities, and intolerance, and the superficiality, and my spiritual needs weren't being met. It would be easy for me to say that. Anyone can take a lot of potshots at Mormons that way. I would not say that it was those things, however, which took me away from the church. Perhaps they played a part.

"I think Mormons have a lot of good things going for them, institutionally and organizationally as well as with the gospel. I love the angel stuff and the idea of revelation. I feel a warmth with those people. These are people that have shortcomings just like I do. . . . I have this huge blind spot, and it worries me—I probably can't come near the truth of the matter of why I left the church."

I have discussed some of the criticisms that came from the respondents who still maintain that they are Mormon. Some were critical of the way the LDS church maintained power and control, their legalism, and their exertion of dominance. Some were critical of the one true church concept, divine guidance and human fallibility, excommunication, and historical inconsistencies. Treatment of both women and African Americans comes under fire, as well as the LDS position on psychotherapy and recent attempts by the church to be acknowledged as a mainstream religion.

The following chapter looks in depth at the wounds the respondents who still retain an LDS identity experienced and their attempts to heal them.

5 Healing the Wounds

The respondents who expressed criticism of the church have been wounded. Many of them have sought ways to heal those wounds, frequently through new belief systems or behaviors.

Six of the seven respondents who currently identify themselves as Mormons show signs of being wounded in their relationship with the LDS church. This is evidenced by pain, anger, and a lack of assertiveness—an unwillingness to talk about their beliefs with current active members of the church. Those with children admit that without LDS guiding principles they have nothing to teach their children, and those who have not discovered a replacement value system such as is present in Christianity still have nothing to teach them. How are these people healing these wounds? How are they working through their grief about the loss of the LDS church's prominent position in their lives? The Christian counselor, Dave Heikkela, pastor of Calvary Agape Fellowship in Ogden, Utah, admits to treating former Mormons as persons in the process of grieving. He employs grief counseling techniques to guide them through their grief.

But what do the questioning Mormons or former Mormons do to heal without the structure and/or resources of traditional Christianity? Sandra Tanner believes that "Mormonism sets people up to be either agnostic or New Age followers." In his interview, Richard gave a comment that illustrates her point: "I describe myself as a secular humanist, naturalist, agnostic, more of a doubter. I'm not going to simply shift allegiance to another value system, another belief system. As the author and explorer Sir Richard Burton said in the 1850s about Mormons who became disenchanted, 'The tendency is for them not to join another church, because once you've believed in an absolute value system and you find it untrue, you don't race off into another one which is going to be untrue.'"[1] This is a valuable insight for understanding the predicament of Mormons in transition.

In this chapter, I discuss the wounds of the six self-identified Mormons and the solutions they've found. The seventh, Alyce Covey, appears to have an unusual capacity for acceptance. She appears to have little pain in her relationship with the Mormon church. However, I must note that on several occasions during the interview, when I asked a question that called for a feeling response, Alyce answered with a thinking answer. I rephrased the question and again got no feeling response. Alyce is either not in touch with her feelings or very private about sharing them. This would account for some of her observed capacity for acceptance.

New Age Ideas

Karen Clark was kicked out of a Sunday school class for her honesty. The event happened on "Fast Sunday" (see *fast and testimony meetings* in the glossary) when her class was given an opportunity to bear their testimonies. When it was Karen's turn, she asked, "I want to know how you can honestly say, 'I know this to be the true church,' parroting what we were taught as children. I can't say that, and I really want to be able to. How do you do it?" Her question set off a landslide of kids getting up to say the same thing. They didn't know how to know if the gospel was true either. The teacher offered no solution to their dilemma. As Karen recounted, "The teacher got very angry. He made everybody be totally quiet. And he told me to leave the room, that I was a Jezebel . . . and that I was poisoning the minds of . . . the boys and girls. I was crushed, heartbroken. And I again felt lonely, isolated, and I didn't fit in."

Karen's turning point in her relationship with her religion came when she was planning to have a patriarchal blessing. Patriarchal blessings are given by a man designated by the LDS church to have inspired vision about the future and the past. Active members see patriarchs as guides who help them live a righteous life. As Karen was making plans to have her blessing, she "felt the blessing would be very, very meaningful. It would be a turning point in my life." But when Karen told her mother about her plans, her mother objected, saying that Karen was too young to have the blessing and that it wouldn't be meaningful. Karen's mother canceled the appointment. Once again, Karen was crushed. She concluded, "Well, that's that. . . . I had felt very strongly that whatever happened around the blessing would be a turning point in my life—and it was."

Karen was always a seeker and she looked for the most part into non-Christian disciplines. As she said, "Along the way, I got the idea that God was love, and I remember having a strong conversation with a great aunt about fearing God. I remember telling her that if she had to have a God she had to fear, then it wasn't going to be my God. . . . God was loving and not terrifying. I feel the Mormon God is a fearful God, a person-God like a parent." All people base their original relationship with God on their relationship with their parents. Unless they uncover and discard this basis, it usually continues for life. Karen discarded a parental God without realizing the source of this belief as she matured.

Although Karen has engaged beliefs commonly called New Age, she objects strongly to the expression on the grounds that there is nothing new about the beliefs. Historian Ruth Tucker agrees: "The most popular and widely publicized new religion in recent years has been the New Age Movement, a difficult-to-define variety of mystical, spiritualistic, and occultic groups that above all else are not *new*. . . . Indeed the response to the New Age is as varied as the Movement itself."[2] But in this discussion I am going to label most of the self-centered—that is, feelings and experience-centered—spiritual beliefs and practices "New Age." Despite her objection, Karen's beliefs fit the category.

Karen described her dilemma regarding what she should teach her children in the absence of the LDS church. "I was beginning to learn where spirituality and morality [were], and that religion and morality were not synonymous. And that was like the beginning of another big awakening. . . . I didn't want religion to ruin their spirituality, their relationship with God. . . . I found aspects that I taught them, universal truths."

Karen finally settled on theosophy, an American version of Eastern religions now centered in India, as the core of her new religion. As we talked and reviewed a theosophy periodical, Karen told me that one of their fundamental propositions healed all her wounds: "#3. Recognition of the unique value of every living being expresses itself in reverence for life, compassion for all, sympathy with the need of all individuals to find truth for themselves, and respect for all religious traditions. The ways in which these ideals become realities in individual life are both the privileged choice and the responsible act of every human being."

It is easy to see that Karen would find these words healing, giving her the freedom to seek truth and to worship as she pleases.

"I think it would be comforting to me to have membership in an organized religion," said Lena. She explained that she had attended both the Methodist and Unity churches because she "wanted an organized religion that would fit me, where women could hold the priesthood, be the prophet, that wasn't just praying to God the Father, but to God the Mother, that wasn't so patriarchal, that was balanced."

Obviously, Lena has moved a good way toward the New Age Movement. She wants a church that fits her beliefs rather than accepting the already defined beliefs and practices of another religion. When I asked Lena where she would go after death, she replied, "Oh, that's not determined by the church you go to. My spiritual program is actually my therapy [Jungian] and my twelve-step program [Overeaters Anonymous, in which she has lost over one hundred pounds], where I feel much closer to God."

I questioned Lena about her renewed attendance at LDS church services and her expressed desire to go to the temple, something only the most conforming Mormons are allowed to do. She replied, "It's like I'm still making up my mind, like I want to keep my options open. Maybe I want to go back to the temple to see what it feels like." She used an analogy of people getting divorced with short reconciliations. "Maybe I'm going to finally divorce the church. I don't know. Or maybe I'm going to stay and go and be my own kind of Mormon, because those men can say what they like and I'm still my own person. . . . I don't want to have my thinking screwed with by them."

Lena, like Karen, is looking for the freedom to decide for herself.

Alan also brings the New Age to Mormonism in the healing of his wounds. "One of the primary attractions of Mormonism for me is its open-endedness and its fluidity . . . this idea of progression, that things change with God and man. You open the door to never being certain about anything. I enjoy that idea. . . . I like the feeling of awe and wonder and mystery. . . . More is to be revealed. . . . I think that is a central aspect of Mormonism, if not *the* central aspect. . . . Things change and are ongoing and are fluid and open-ended." Alan wears a different pair of glasses in his look at the LDS church. Where others see domination and control, Alan sees immense freedom. And here is his belief that makes this possible: "Although, given the openness of the gospel, a direct clash in doctrine seems improbable. Were this to occur, then you trust your private experience rather than any institutional edict." His trust of experience is his way out of being a conforming Mormon, or accepting beliefs that he finds unacceptable.

Wayne was not wounded by the LDS church, but his conversion *out* of the LDS church on a spiritual level did injure his wife. As he reports, "It was devastating, . . . the ground just fell underneath her." At that point he made a life-directing decision: "That since this [deconversion] experience hadn't grown out of my own personal pain or dissatisfaction with anything, that there was no good to be accomplished by my trying to disturb other people." He made a decision to answer all questions honestly, but not to offer up his beliefs. This was made for the sake of his children, because, as he said, "I really didn't have something specific to offer them as a substitute."

Wayne is no stranger to taking stands on other issues that affect people in the community, but they are always seen by him as working toward the highest good. About his decision toward passivity with respect to his family and the church, Wayne commented, "Unless there was some extraordinary good that could result from my making a couple of activist stands . . ." He followed wistfully with, "If I thought that my presence in the church would make a difference . . ." He could answer neither of those implied questions affirmatively.

Upon finding some fault with the LDS church, the majority of questioning Mormons interviewed expressed an initial desire to stay in the church and try to make a difference. Most finally gave up and left active participation.

I interviewed Wayne in his well-stocked library. According to Wayne, "The Bible is not the only sacred book." He is well read in the world's religions, about which he said, "I always find things that make it impossible for me to practice, to be disciplined in the way of traditional adherents. We are almost forced into making our own. Making one's own spiritual practice is not so easy. . . . I sympathize with Mormons who want a package that is easier to deal with than rolling your own—which is not easy."

He surmises that this difficulty may have something to do with the LDS church. "You don't just shed your religious tradition when you are seeking your own. . . . I don't want to put those important prerogatives into the hands of other people." It's hard to change religious practice.

Agnosticism

Larry DuBois could be called a spiritually committed agnostic, and much of that stems from his experience with the Mormon church. He said, "I've never spent five minutes in my entire life—I mean literally five minutes—searching for a church to fill the hole left by the Mormon church. I have always been a searcher and a questor, and I have always been looking for something to fill that hole. But I have not spent five minutes trying to fill it with another religion. I assume that came from my hostility and my sense of the institutional hypocrisy—the money, property, and prestige that I sense coming from the Mormon church."

Larry added, "I'm certain there are loads of very nice people in the church. I don't mean to belittle them, the very ordinary Mormon people. My anger is directed to two groups: the one nobody's heard of—the one that runs it—the power behind the power behind the power. And the other group . . . the authorities who inflict control on ordinary people and, therefore, are being intellectually dishonest with themselves."

Our last conversation centered on Larry's looking for the source of his anger. He started out, "Don't you guys get it, that you've been brainwashed, absolutely, stone brainwashed!" I asked Larry what caused his anger. Was it that they continue trying to brainwash others? "I think so," Larry said. "Because that's evil. You can have compassion for their being brainwashed, but for spreading it, that's another story."

Richard talked about the source of his wound: "My goal was to strengthen my gospel knowledge and belief, taking pretty literally the church's scriptural invitation to study out of the best, experiment upon his faith, and all that." Richard took that seriously and started reading history, looking at documents in archives, at the State Historical Society, and at Brigham Young University. He began writing as well as reading and "slowly determined that [the LDS church] wasn't as it had represented itself to be in all the important categories."

Richard went on with an analogy: "It was a slow process. I would compare it to the scales of justice. At one point, at one time in my life, the sands were all on the side of orthodoxy. And then the sand moved over to the side called heterodoxy. Sometime, in the middle of the night . . . the scales tipped and just kept tipping." He finished with, "So it took years, because I never wanted to disbelieve. I wanted to believe more not less."

This tipping of the scales bore consequences in terms of family, friends, and his business. "I have written some things that are not overtly anti-Mormon but were reform oriented—pointing toward problems and identifying possible solutions." This, he explained, put him in the category of apostate. "The church has a way of narrowing the spectrum of orthodoxy to the very narrowest boundary. If you fit in it, you're okay, and if you fit outside . . . if you're very far outside the spectrum of belief, then they cut you off."

Richard has the same laissez-faire attitude as Wayne regarding his children. "I will support them in their religious yearnings whatever they are, wherever they lead them." Richard chose to heal by staying in the church and attempting to communicate. This had positive and negative effects. Richard explained, "But it's a strange thing in Utah for the heterodox Mormon, or the lapsed Mormon, because the gentiles don't trust you—you're too Mormon for them. And the orthodox Mormons don't trust you—you're too heretical for them. So you end up being in this sort of limbo." He described the pain as subtle, "not a biting, stinging sharp pain. It's a dull day-to-day sort of thing, where you realize you're different, and they look at you differently. There are subtle kinds of discrimination on all sides that go on. You're sort of shunned in an almost imperceptible way. But you can feel it. . . . That's just the price of leaving and staying."

An examination of these respondents' attempts to heal reveals two points: The respondents continue to make decisions based on their personal experience after leaving active believer status as Mormons, and they seem to end up going in a New Age direction or becoming, as Larry and Richard are, agnostics.

I personally became an agnostic, New Age practitioner. But I had a problem with this practice and the LDS church that I just couldn't resolve. I was perplexed by a statement by a guru of mine: "If you were raised to marry a good Jewish girl, you will never find contentment until you marry a good Jewish girl." By this time, I had become convinced of the inaccuracies of LDS dogma and history. My dilemma was: Am I to give up my personal integrity and attend the church? or, Am I never to find contentment? I found my answer in letting go of my subconscious belief in the LDS church's claims of being the one true church.

6

Those Captured by Christianity

The previous chapter presented the coping mechanisms employed by disenchanted or wounded Mormons. All of these strategies were also employed at some time in the lives of each of the traditional Christian respondents discussed in this chapter. However, members of this group ultimately experienced healing through traditional Christianity.

The respondents to these interviews were not, in general, attracted to traditional Christianity. As Richard quoted Sir Richard Burton in the last chapter (here paraphrased): When people find one absolute belief system wrong, they are loathe to rush off to find a new one. Any attraction to Christianity that these people felt occurred early in the process of leaving. But this attraction was more an awakening to differences in belief rather than a desire to make Christianity a part of their lives. Having uncovered problems with the LDS church, most disenchanted Mormons were adjusting to their collapsing worldview. They had little energy left to investigate other alternatives. The discovery that Christians did not necessarily fit the description supplied by the Mormon church was merely a single step in the process of leaving the LDS church. Indeed, it appears that the former-Mormon Christians I interviewed were captured by rather than attracted to Christianity. They were not looking for the Jesus of the Bible, but *he* found *them*. The initiative came from outside their conscious awareness.

Conversion Stories

Tim Schmall was invited to the office of a man who showed him the movie *The Godmakers*.[1] Tim said, "It completely destroyed any hope of Mormonism being the right one. It shattered everything. I was broken and weeping. . . . If that's true, then why do I even exist? If my end is not to become a god, why do I exist? . . . That's all I knew by the time that film was over."

But then, as Tim reported, the man followed with, "If you want to go to heaven all you have to do is ask Jesus to take you on, and he will."

"When he said that," Tim said, "my heart just screamed yes. My mind said, 'How can it be that simple?' My heart said, 'It is. Just believe.' I believed and accepted the Lord, right there, and it was just incredible. It was like I was washed clean."

Will McGarvey talked about the way God works with us. "That's the amazing thing about Christianity. It's not just, 'Follow this set of rules'—this works-type thing. . . . It's being purchased and having a relationship, a love affair with

God." Will admits to having difficulties still with that relationship: "Am I still going to have a relationship with Jesus Christ? For some reason God kept in my heart that I needed that relationship. . . . The Holy Spirit inspires people to stay on this path that God placed them on."

> Bryan Ohlsen is an enthusiastic twenty-one-year-old, an intense and dedicated former Mormon. Bryan has been active in politics for several years. He's a doer and a leader.
>
> My impression is that Bryan is driven to achieve, and it will take a few years for him to mellow out. Mormonism stresses success in the world and worldly achievement. It takes time to lose that intense drive. Bryan says that he already has experienced some of the mellowing process since being captured by the Lord.
>
> He is married, and he and his wife have produced a packet on how to get one's name taken off the rolls of the LDS church.

Bryan Ohlsen, the high school debater, was taken by the Lord through Bible studies. Bryan examined all the traditional Mormon proof texts in light of the whole chapter in which they were written using the standard, Christian method of exegesis. He found a different interpretation than the Mormons teach. He continued his research afterward. "I started reading Bible studies. I prayed about it. It was the most incredible experience I ever had in my life. It was like hitting a brick wall. I was praying. I said, 'Christ, take over my life. I want to believe. Help me to believe.' I fell to the ground, and I couldn't move, and all I could do was cry. I don't know how long I lay there unable to move." Bryan says that this experience was important for him. "I needed that. I needed to be shook up. I needed to know for sure that the decision I had made was correct. And just that instance alone is proof to me." Mormons are instructed to be validated by emotional experiences. For Bryan this experience was compelling.

Brittany Fyans, too, was captured while reading the Bible. She had a boyfriend who had been telling her that she just needed to let go, to quit analyzing everything. "Just let it happen. Read the Bible for a couple of months." And so that's what Brittany was doing. "I was reading the Bible—tearing it apart. . . . Then I just let go. It was like God was inside of me, saying, 'Just let go. Let me into your life. Invite me into your life.' I just said, 'I commit my life to you.'" As she did that, Brittany said, "I felt like a balloon blew up. Like wow, I exist! I'm okay. I'm so accepted, so full. It was like knowledge. A veil was lifted from a whole bunch of knowledge." Though Brittany couldn't tell what the knowledge was, her questions were gone, and she now had conviction.

Lynda Cooley also credits the Lord for bringing her to him. "The Lord started working on me a long time before I accepted him. I remember the Campus Crusade people coming to my house and really listening to them about a year before I got saved. When I actually got saved, I went to visit a friend in San Diego. When I got there, I began asking her questions. We stayed up all night. And I accepted the Lord. It was purely my pulling it out of her." But Lynda doesn't take credit for the pullings. "I was just ready. The Lord had prepared me a long time before."

Ross Anderson is a thirty-nine-year-old Evangelical Free pastor, whose family accepted his leaving the LDS church as a phase he was going through, until he told them about his decision to go to a seminary and study for the ministry.

Ross was raised in California, where one finds few exclusively cultural Mormons attending church services. Most California Mormons view themselves as part of a much more dedicated body than those in the Mormon-dominated intermountain region of the western states.

Ross has recovered his relationship with his family and is on good terms with a brother-in-law who is a faculty member at BYU, as well as with many nieces and nephews attending that university.

Ross Anderson had considered himself a Christian at the time of his conversion. "I thought of myself as a Christian. I called myself a Christian. And I had some emerging understanding of things that I had picked up along the way." He had been attending a liturgical church. Then all that changed. "I met someone I was working with at college who was a genuine Christian, and to her the things I said did not ring true. She invited me to begin attending worship with her. This was a Bible teaching church. . . . I saw the difference, with that sermon, about where my life was going and what Jesus offered. . . ." When confronted with this difference, Ross accepted. "I'd tried one thing after another. I made that night a conscious decision to surrender my life to Christ and to trust him to do something with me." And as Ross completed this story, "There was nothing in the program, not an evangelical appeal. God had just brought me to that point."

Cindy Lou Blackmon spoke about how casually she accepted an invitation from a friend to attend her church. "A lady at work had been bugging me to go to her church. I did, and the pastor preached on Psalm 139. I had never heard anything like that before—ever in my whole life. That's when I realized that the LDS church isn't true." Cindy later responded to the question, "How did you begin to seek other ways of relating to God?" with, "Only when I discovered who he was. At that time, he had swept my house clean. It was empty, and I was just waiting. He put Christians around me, and I thought they were so beautiful. I just couldn't get enough of them. And I know that he did that on purpose, because there's not a lot of those kind of people around."

I previously mentioned Christine Campbell's invitation to a Women's Aglow meeting. As Christine reported, "I was whisked into that meeting. There were hands on me. I felt God's gentleness." She could hear Jesus saying to her, "I am your Savior. I was with you when you were a little, tiny child, and I'm still here. I love you." Christine went on, "I was instantly saved then. I just can't get enough. I'm taking in everything I possibly can. There is nothing on this earth that can compare with the love I feel. Words just don't describe it."

> Tawna Robinson is a forty-one-year-old mother of three who came to the Lord before questioning the LDS church at all. Her conversion experience occurred while she was in college.
>
> Tawna has been an active Christian leader and a teacher of "Precepts Training" (an inductive method of Bible study) throughout the Wasatch Range.
>
> Tawna is married to an inactive baptized Mormon. He is reluctant to have his name removed from the rolls, so neither has taken any action on this matter.

Tawna Robinson described her conversion experience. She says she was walking with a new friend who lived in her dorm at Utah State University. "We were walking back [to the dorm] and saw a couple fighting. I said, 'There must be some way that people can live together and be happy.' And he said, 'There is.' He spoke with such assurance. I said, 'How?' He said, 'With Jesus Christ.' I started weeping, right there on the spot. I didn't know why. He hit a respondent cord." She met with that new friend later that night, went over the four spiritual laws,[2] and "received the Lord sitting on the cold concrete, sitting on the steps of the Union Building." Tawna invited Jesus into her life: "Jesus,

come into my life. Take it all over. I've made a mess of it."
She remembers what happened after that prayer: "I remember feeling the Holy Spirit just trickle from my head
to my toes and just lift me. It was a physical rejuvenation.
God gave me what I had been seeking. And I just felt like
I was about three feet off the ground. I was like a teapot
constantly boiling over, but there was no way that I could
contain the joy."

The Process of Coming to Christ

This process of accepting Christ as Lord and personal
Savior is what is meant by "coming to Christ." Others refer
to this as being "born again," based on Jesus' admonition
to Nicodemus, "I tell you the truth, no one can see the kingdom of God unless he is born again" (John 3:3 NIV). And
yet others, who use the New Revised Standard Version,
translate that passage "born from above." But nonetheless,
we are talking about a decision to follow Jesus, as revealed
in the Bible alone.

Unfortunately, for the reasons described in the preced-
ing chapters, an admittedly small segment of those leaving
the LDS church actually worship Christ as Lord and Savior. Some leave active membership but still think of themselves and describe themselves as Mormons (Larry, Alan).
Others leave active membership more completely without
taking their names off the church rolls (Richard). Even those
who are nonbelievers may participate in church activities
(Wayne, Alyce Covey, Lena). Many who leave their names
on the rolls participate in other "spiritual disciplines" (Karen
Clark), while still others become agnostic or atheistic
(Wayne, Richard). Having belonged to the "one true church"
tends to limit investigation of other denominations.

I believe that having a personal relationship with the
Christ of the Bible will rid one of the grief felt at leaving the

comfort of the LDS church. I found no peace until Christ captured me for his kingdom. And I was the most unwilling of believers. I was brought kicking and screaming into his arms. It was only through God's bounteous grace that I was called. I did absolutely nothing to earn my salvation. I wasn't looking for it. It was a free gift. I didn't even understand the meaning of the term *salvation* when I accepted Jesus' call. And it was more than a year before the vocabulary of traditional Christianity began to make any sense to me. Nonetheless, I was his.

My conversion experience happened walking back to my office from a fast food restaurant where I had been confronted by a born-again Christian. He asked me to investigate my relationship with Jesus. I knew that would be easy. I had none—Jesus was just part of the whole myth of Mormonism. Leaving the restaurant, I asked what I called my God voice what that relationship was, and I got the response, "Who do you think you've been talking to?"

I invite you now to pause and look at your life. I invite you to look into your experience and then ask God if there is truth to what has been spoken here. I invite you to ask Jesus to come into your life. It can be as simple as saying this simple prayer:

> Dear Lord Jesus,
> I know that I am a sinner (have preferred my way to yours) and need your forgiveness. I believe that you died for my sins. I invite you to come into my heart and life. I want to trust and follow you as Lord and Savior.
>
> In Jesus' name, Amen.

Listening to these experiences in this chapter, both originally and again on tape, living with this material, transcribing it, reading it time after time, have been among the most meaningful experiences of my life. It has been a privilege for me to be in the presence of God, who captured these people for his kingdom.

The next chapter deals with the experiences of transition for those persons who were converted to follow Jesus, both the change in their worldview and how they dealt with that change. The process of leaving the LDS church gives many opportunities for growth. Some of us run from those opportunities, hiding in alcoholism (as I did), eating disorders, addiction to prescribed medication, or other addictions. But eventually, if we are to live full and complete lives, we must face these challenges by continuing on the road of personal growth.

I investigated in my research the continued growth challenges offered to former Mormons converted to follow the biblical Jesus. It is not an easy road. We have to confront how very different our theological bases are as well as our forms of worship.

7

A Change in Worldview

The process of changing one's worldview is difficult. It is especially disorienting for new Christian converts from the LDS church. The words used by Mormons and Christians are frequently the same, but the meanings of those words are different. As Mormons, these converts believed that the Bible was the Word of God "as far as it is translated correctly."[1] And they believed that they were getting a valid interpretation of the Bible. But the LDS church has a lay pastorate, and, therefore, the body of the LDS church is untrained in the exegesis of Scripture. The LDS "proof texts" are frequently taken out of the context in which they were written, and as a result, the meaning attributed to these Scriptures by the reader is not the meaning intended at the time of writing. The converts had also believed that the Book of Mormon was the word of God. Most converts from Mormonism to traditional Christianity, and, therefore, to a biblical point of view, discover that their relationship to the Word of God is quite confused. Clarifying that relationship can take years.

Christian Respondents' Observations

One respondent, Cindy Lou Blackmon, talked about her disorientation during the process of transition: "I remember being frustrated when I first became a Christian—being so frustrated when I'd read the Bible. Trying to sort out what I had read in the Book of Mormon with what I was reading in the Bible. I would call the pastor and say, 'Are the ten tribes still lost?' [A foundational doctrine of the LDS church is that the American continents were populated by peoples from two of the ten lost tribes of Israel.] He'd laugh and say, 'No, the ten tribes were never lost.' One day, in frustration, I just sat down and prayed, 'God, you've just got to take away the Mormon doctrine.' And that's why I didn't pick up the Book of Mormon until last year, after a five-year hiatus. I separated myself from it all so that I could concentrate on the truth. Now I think I'm at a stage where I can go back to it and see the difference."

Sandra Tanner, too, remembers difficulty sorting out differences in beliefs between the LDS church and biblical Christianity: "I remember the day that I accepted Christ. I sat in my front room. . . . If I'm not a Mormon, what do I believe? What do I believe now that I didn't believe five minutes ago? What does it mean to not be a Mormon anymore? It took time to work that through." Sandra went to the Bible. "I started reading through the Bible trying to figure out what I was *taught* that isn't true and which things [just] aren't true. That was a long process. . . . [I] read the

Bible. I had to think things through. 'Is that a Mormon interpretation or a Christian interpretation? See how much of your life has been tainted by this philosophy.' [This process] gave [me] a new worldview."[2]

While forty-three-year-old Christine Campbell had not attended the LDS church since the age of nineteen, she still considered herself a Mormon. It was through a charismatic experience at a Women's Aglow meeting that she came to the Lord.

Christine has a Ph.D. in psychology and recently started taking classes at Utah Institute for Biblical Study,[3] an evangelical Christian school. Christine has never married.

Christine still struggles with trying to find out what Christians believe: "The difficulty that I'm finding is [discovering] what the Christian doctrines are compared to what I think they are." Because LDS doctrine is a tightly controlled body of thought and the LDS church is hierarchical, members are told what to believe. Christine thought that Christian doctrine would be handed to her in the same way.

In his interview, Will McGarvey pointed out how important it is to grapple with the doctrinal differences: "As we grapple with these issues, [investigators] can go either way. Mormons tend to see questioning as something leading them away from their faith and the one true church. . . . When you look from a faith perspective, the only way our faith grows is when we grapple with issues. . . . Grappling allows our faith to grow. [Faith] doesn't stand still. It either grows or dwindles." The opportunity to ask questions is a new concept for disaffected Mormons. Rather than accepting "revealed" doctrine, as Christians they are not only allowed to question, they are encouraged to question.

Doctrinal Issues

The respondents found some doctrinal issues more difficult to accept or reject than others.

Eternal Progression

Active Mormons live with an essentially comforting worldview, a portion of which is supplied by their prophet. Joseph Smith taught that we all existed as spirit children of God before our birth on earth. For the most dedicated followers, life here is only a step in an eternal progression toward becoming gods of our own worlds. All that is required is obedience to the "commandments." If a Mormon does not qualify for future godhood (or does not become the wife of a god), he or she will still be comfortable in whichever of the three levels of heaven he or she attains.

Giving up this view of mortality as a passage between a preexistence and a three-tiered heaven (I again refer you to fig. 1) can be the most difficult doctrine for a disaffected Mormon to reject. The plan of eternal progression is taught beginning in early childhood.

When Tawna Robinson was asked which LDS doctrine was most difficult to give up, she immediately answered, "The preexistence and the post-existence were the hardest. New believers [in the biblical Jesus] are given information about simple things—grace and salvation. But [our teachers] don't address what happens to us before we came. And heaven is even vague in the Bible."

Tawna experienced confusion when comparing the LDS doctrine of eternal progression with the biblical teaching of salvation by grace: "Things would come back at me, and I wouldn't be able to sort out whether it was Mormon or biblical. It seemed like for five years after, I knew I needed to immerse myself in the Bible. . . . After five years

I could say that preexistence is Mormon not biblical. I had kept trying to find it in the Bible." She also looked for information regarding the three degrees of glory: "Also, levels in heaven. It was hard to give up because it fit in so logically with the 'works' orientation. There was an answer to what's going to happen after we die. In the Bible, it's much more vague. Especially right at first [after conversion], I didn't study that kind of stuff. No one sat me down and did a topical study on heaven." Christine Campbell, too, mentioned that "the afterlife, families in the hereafter, and eternal marriage" were the hardest LDS principles to give up.

Bryan Ohlsen, commenting on this subject, said, "The plan of eternal progression was so instilled in my head. I had to believe in the celestial kingdom because I didn't believe in heaven and hell." There are corollary doctrines as well, some of which Bryan pointed out: "I had to believe that God has a purpose for me in this life. I was too up on myself and too confident in myself to believe that God had just put me here. I believed that he had something in mind for me—that I had existed for a while."

Tim Schmall, too, spoke in particular about the attachment of Mormon males to the concept of eternal progression: "That men can become gods. I don't care what these men say, that is their driving force behind everything. . . . That's the foundation of everything." He spoke about his demeanor while holding that belief: "I was very smug, carried myself with a regal bearing, condescending, patronizing." He talked about his process of letting go of LDS teachings and accepting Bible-based doctrines. He identified the doctrine of eternal progression as central to his LDS belief system: "Once I let that go, everything else just fell to pieces. . . . Nothing else really mattered."

The Godhead

Bryan Ohlsen and Tim Schmall struggled with their concepts of God. Bryan said, "I had to believe that God was a man. I had to believe that God was three separate entities." And Tim commented on how hard it was to accept the biblical view of God: "It was difficult for me to come to the point where I understood that I would never understand. When I got that, it was a piece of cake."

Will McGarvey mentioned "the mystery of the Trinity." He spoke about the "awesome, majestic God who calls us into relationship with him. That's the amazing thing that Christianity is. It's not just following a set of rules, this works-type thing. . . . It's being purchased and having a relationship—a love affair with God. That was real tough because I had always seen God as this real distant being on the planet Kolob. God was physical. It was hard to overcome." According to Mormon scripture, God resides on the planet Kolob. The *Pearl of Great Price* contains "The Book of Abraham" in which Joseph Smith explains his teaching concerning the plurality of gods. In it he also talks about preexistence and introduces Kolob (Abr. 3:2–18).

Russ Lane still struggles with the Trinity: "I still have kind of a Reorganized Latter-day Saint doctrine on that.[4] God is a spirit. But I feel that the physical manifestation of Jesus made him separate from God. . . . I have not been able to reconcile myself to that. It's probably why I'm an American Baptist. They have room for me to have different opinions." Russ shared his concept of the Trinity: "God the Father, who's Spirit; the son, Jesus Christ, who's resurrected and has a physical body and is separate from God; and the Holy Spirit is the spiritual influence in the mind of God influencing in the world." Russ went on to explain: "It doesn't fit with Mormonism's [belief] or with most Christians. I don't teach that doctrine, but if people ask what I believe, I tell them."

Will, like Russ, also noted his need to find "a more liberal church. A church that stresses soul freedom rather than conformity. . . . Coming from such a dogmatic, authoritarian tradition, I needed to learn that God and myself work together . . . have the freedom to continue to grow, to start the transformation process." Will has since moved to a Presbyterian church with a strong evangelical stance.

Gender Roles

> Evah Bigler is a sixty-year-old woman who came to Christ as a result of leaving Salt Lake City ten years ago, when she got to know non-Mormons. She states that she believes in the Bible's accuracy much more than her pastor preaches.
>
> She was converted after her husband's conversion, but on her own. Criticism of her conversion experience caused her to be unwilling to share it with anyone.
>
> Evah reports that she and her husband have made several unsuccessful attempts to have their names removed from the LDS church rolls, the final public acknowledgment of their apostasy from Mormonism.

For Evah Bigler the biggest adjustment to traditional Christianity was to "women pastors, elders, deacons, etc.," because the LDS hierarchy consists only of men, and only men hold the priesthood. Women gain their place in the hereafter through marriage.

> Brittany Fyans is a vivacious and talkative twenty-five-year-old, whose womanhood put her in conflict with the Mormon church. In my opinion, Brittany was never meant to be a typical, submissive, Mormon wife. She has too much energy and too much to accomplish in life.

> Although she had a profound conversion experience three years ago and has not attended the LDS church for the last six, Brittany still struggles with giving up the Book of Mormon and other doctrinal issues.

Brittany Fyans struggled with gender roles associated with the LDS church. "The sexuality of the LDS church was hard for me—that we were females and males before we came to the earth, because I'm a person who is offended by sexuality in the world today. . . . I don't like to see it as, 'You're a man and I'm a woman.' I've never accepted that, because I've never felt like a woman the way the Mormon church defines them—that I'm going to be closest to God when I'm pregnant. . . . My place is in the home. I've never related to that. It never made any sense to me."

But she laments, "When my life isn't plastic and perfect, I think, 'Oh, if I was in the Mormon church, everything would be plastic and perfect.' But I'm not envious of that," she says, calling on her experience of what LDS women have to give up in order to have a life with that appearance. They have to be out of touch with their "real selves," which is evidenced by the fact that many Utah women are addicted to mood-altering prescription drugs. In the *Network* article "Closet Addictions, Utah Women Hooked on Prescription Drugs," Gode Davis states, "It is an illicit and physician-condoned epidemic, more pervasive than the use of 'crack' cocaine and heroin combined. It is also a pernicious dependency masked by cultural denial."[5]

Nondoctrinal Issues

The respondents had problems adjusting to Christianity for reasons other than doctrinal issues.

Elements of Worship

Bryan Ohlsen had "problems with baptism. Coming from the Mormon religion, I had problems with the organized religion and ceremonial-type things. So I had a hard time with, for example, the Lord's Supper. It was something that I didn't participate in for a long time." Sandra Tanner commented that "some things smacked of Catholicism. As a Mormon, I had been trained to be turned off by anything with the trappings of Catholicism. Just having altar boys go down and light candles . . . passing the offering. We had such deep training against a paid ministry. 'The ministers are just out for your money. Just a money grab.' Passing the offering plate was so offensive, so blatant."

Sense of Community

Lynda Cooley is a forty-nine-year-old special education teacher in the Granite School District just south of Salt Lake City. She has a grown but still dependent autistic son.

Of all those interviewed, she spent the longest time away from organized religion. She was raised by inactive parents in a very active Mormon extended family.

Lynda is the Sunday school superintendent at her church. She is trying to decide between a Wycliffe ministry, teaching the children of missionaries, and entering a Ph.D. program in special education that she has been invited to join. Finding care for her son will be the deciding factor.

Lynda Cooley mentioned, as did almost all of my respondents, the pain of being cut off from family: "All of my relatives [are] good Mormons. Whenever there's a wedding, a baptism, a baby being blessed, it all revolves around the Mormon church. Or someone going on a mission. At all of those things, I'm kind of an outcast. I feel it. But I really don't have contact with them all the time. It's just at big family get-togethers. They're all talking about church things, and I'm not involved in that, so I'm not a part of that."

Niki Payne, too, spoke about the loss of community: "Fellowship with Christians in other organizations has not been compensation for the loss of community, because a scar is left by Mormonism. I am reluctant to trust organizations or large groups where my individual needs and conscience might be sacrificed for the good of the group." Niki acknowledged this as "a necessary loss." She was the only respondent to mention that it was difficult to give up "the basic belief that the LDS church is 'the only true, living church on the face of the earth.'"

Trust

In addition to doctrinal issues such as eternal progression, the nature of the godhead, eternal gender roles, and issues regarding elements of worship and community, former Mormons frequently find it difficult to trust. They feel betrayed, and it is often difficult to rehabilitate their capacities to trust.[6] Niki finished her interview by saying, "The hardest doctrine to accept was the wonder and mystery of God's love for me. His incarnation, his atonement, and forgiveness. His omnipotence. And only because it took time for me to trust."

The Pastors' Observations

In addition to the respondents who were former or questioning Mormons, I interviewed five pastors for this book. All five were men and had extensive experience working with former Mormons and those investigating leaving the LDS church. They all admitted they had learned valuable lessons from the mistakes they made while working with these people. All have former Mormons in their congregations. Four of the pastors commented on the difficulties former Mormons have in leaving the LDS church.

Chris Vlachos is the pastor of Calvary Fellowship in American Fork, Utah. Regarding converts' difficulties in adjusting to a new worldview, he observed, "I think initially the hardest thing for [converts] to give up is the eternal family." My survey supports this observation. But Pastor Chris added some clarification: "What they find is that they have a misassumption that Christianity teaches otherwise—that Christians believe that they won't be together. But Christians believe that we will. After we die, we'll see each other again, and there will be eternal fellowship—togetherness in Christ. . . . We'll all be the bride of Christ. We'll also be married for time and eternity in the sense that the church will be married to Christ. So a lot of that stuff we can still maintain. Initially, Mormons had a hard time giving that up. But once they believe that we also believe that there will be conscious fellowship in the afterlife, it softens that." This belief may soften the loss, but Christian conversion still requires a dramatic change in worldview, for with the LDS doctrine of eternal family come the physical qualities of God, the separation of Father, Son, and Holy Spirit, and the potential for practicing Mormons to attain godhead.

Bill Heersink is a Christian Reformed pastor in Ogden, Utah. He spoke about the difficulty in coming to understand what it means to relate to God as "our Father." "Sometimes I feel like we just aren't hearing each other. . . . So often I hear Mormons say, 'God is literally our father'—as if our relationship to him is in every way just like that to our earthly father. 'We belong to the same species with the same genetic markings as God. Just as we have the potential to be everything our human parents have become, so we can grow up to be everything our heavenly Father is now.' To change from that perception to the Christian view is a major paradigm shift."

Jeff Silliman is a Presbyterian pastor in Salt Lake. He talked about how difficult it is for converts to change their conception of the qualities of God: "[Mormons have] the idea of a loving teddy bear kind of father. They don't have much idea of God's holiness. God's kind of a buddy. . . . There's nothing wrong with that—the Abba side. But there's the otherness—they don't have much of a concept of." Pastor Jeff mentioned the absence of "the whole idea of sovereignty of God—that God is the one in absolute control of the universe. They have the idea that God is a 'God fellow,' that he's just down the road a bit from us. We're kind of in the same ballpark."

Pat Edwards, a Baptist pastor in Bountiful, Utah, identified grace versus works as the toughest issue new converts struggle with: "Everything [in LDS doctrine] is so works oriented. Grace, not in the sense of salvation, but grace in life—forgiveness and mercy. The idea that I'm motivated by God's love—by the work of grace in my life, not because I have to. So often [new converts] get involved with things because of that sense of obligation. I think they really wrestle with the freedom that we have in Christ."

All respondents agreed that the change from the LDS to the historical Christian worldview is a difficult one. As Sandra Tanner said, "The first year out of Mormonism was extremely lonely. Without Christ I probably would have drifted back into the [Mormon] social structure." The power of having Jesus present in our lives makes the big difference in handling adjustment difficulties. Without a relationship with Jesus, we would most likely return to the comfort of the LDS church. However, the struggles and difficulties bring us closer to God.

Both the converted former Mormons and the pastors familiar with them agreed that former Mormons coming to the Lord of historical Christianity must make major and difficult changes in worldview. Letting go of the plan of eternal progression and acquiring an understanding of the Trinity are particularly difficult for former Mormons. The loss of a sense of community and the adjustment to new gender roles and forms of Christian worship also gave them great difficulty. But because these converts had previously believed that their own works were essential to their progress, most difficult for them was simply trusting God, surrendering to God's grace.

8

Additional Experiences

As mentioned in the previous chapter, converts from Mormonism to Christianity must adjust their worldview, which requires the acceptance of new doctrinal beliefs. After conversion, former Mormons go through additional experiences, ranging from telling their families of their decision to removing their names from the LDS church roles.

I have not been alone in inquiring into barriers Mormons face in leaving the LDS church and choosing a new faith. Sandra Tanner gave me a paper entitled, "Obstacles to Leaving Mormonism." The following ten assumptions are taken from this paper.

1. The Bible has been corrupted to such a degree that no one can know for sure what it originally said.

2. Therefore, a modern-day prophet is needed to speak for God.
3. If the Mormon prophet is not trustworthy, then we cannot know the truth.
4. Since other churches make contradictory claims, none of them can have the truth.
5. An unbroken line of priesthood ordination from the original Apostles until today is needed in order to act with God's authority.
6. The most reliable knowledge of truth comes from prayer and feelings, not from comparing evidence.
7. Reading anti-Mormon literature does not give you a feeling of peace; therefore, it can't be from God.
8. Since most people are decent, God would not be too harsh with their failures.
9. Almost everyone will be saved in some level of heaven; therefore, there is no ultimate fear of God's judgment.
10. A loving God would make it possible for all his children to be saved. Only Mormonism offers a way to convert the dead who die without hearing the gospel.[1]

Sandra Tanner has had a ministry since 1960, now called Utah Lighthouse Ministries,[2] that assists people investigating leaving the LDS church. She also identified steps that people take in making this transition (see appendix D). The male former Mormons whom I interviewed agreed with the steps more than most of the females.

Will McGarvey was a committed missionary. But it was on his mission that he was challenged by non-Mormons, specifically by a minister from Rhode Island, who, as Will said, "sat through the discussions [the lessons the Mormon missionaries use to convert nonmembers] with his neighbors. We had other discussions afterwards. I was pretty closed minded. . . . He raised implications that were different than I had ever heard. . . . He was talking about grace.

He was talking about salvation." These were new concepts to Will. "[The minister] was talking about a believer's priesthood, that everyone is a priest in the royal family of God. Those who would pretend to hold the Aaronic and Melchizedek priesthood are just pretenders." (The LDS church holds that the Aaronic priesthood was conferred on Joseph Smith by John the Baptist and, later, the Melchizedek priesthood was conferred by Peter, James, and John.) Will continued, "He brought out some pretty striking Scriptures to back up his points. But I was able to rationalize for a while."

Will was also invited to Thanksgiving dinner with a Christian family. This, too, had an impact. "I saw a good model family. I thought they didn't exist outside of Mormonism."

Niki Payne began dating a Mormon boy, whom she wrote to while he was on an LDS mission. During his absence, she also was converted to the LDS church, over the objections, which she could not understand, of her many Baptist friends. She does now. But she "had had a burning bosom experience and was convinced of the truth of the experience and of the Mormon church." She married her missionary upon his return.

Niki's first doubts, discussed in chapter 2, were a result of the lack of the church's response to her depression. Upon studying the Bible, she "found the basic principles of the Christian faith to be in conflict with the LDS way of life and in conflict with LDS doctrine." As she says, "I came to a point where I was willing to submit to God's love for me and to his authority in my life. My loyalty to Mormonism was broken."

When she spoke to her husband about these changes and about her desire to "worship outside the Mormon church," her husband's response was negative. "If I left Mormonism, the marriage was [would be] over." Niki spoke to her bishopric (bishop and his two counselors) and stake presidency (the bishop's supervisor and spiritual overseer along with his two counselors) and was encouraged to remain in the church. As Niki said, "I hoped for some time to remain a member of the church and to be a part of its reformation. But I longed for the nurture of Christian worship and fellowship." Eventually she and her husband were divorced. It was at that point that she started attending a traditional Christian church.

Brittany Fyans presents a fairly typical case. She has not attended an LDS church meeting for the past six years. She acknowledges that she has been a born-again Christian for almost three years, and yet she is still unwilling to cut her ties to the Mormon church. While she attends a traditional Christian church and teaches Sunday school there, she is still seeking answers to many of her questions. As did Sandra Tanner, she is still holding on to the Book of Mormon. Brittany mused, "What if the Book of Mormon is based on real records? There's real poetry in there. You can't say that Joseph Smith is bright enough to put something like that together. . . . I don't know."

She reflected, "I haven't been to the Mormon church since I was nineteen, but I haven't made a commitment to leave." This conflict appears to be typical, for women in particular. For example, Tawna Robinson has been a devout and active traditional Christian for twenty-two years, but she still has not taken the step to have her name removed from the rolls. Evah Bigler reported having unsuccessfully tried several times to make a final break by having her name removed from the rolls. As Brittany said about having her name taken off the rolls, "There is something in me that doesn't want to. . . . All my past is Mormon. It would feel as if I didn't exist. Get rid of my childhood. Throw away all my pictures."

Brittany compared that nothingness with the security of the LDS church: "The Mormon church seems solid—like really solid. Maybe that's because it's my core belief. It's my Rock of Gibraltar. It's solid and big and massive." Obviously, it's hard to leave. Although I asked no questions about having one's name removed from the church rolls, many of the respondents spoke about it.

Cindy Lou Blackmon mentioned her anger regarding the reliability of both prophecy and feelings, anger turned inward *and* outward. Less than half of the respondents mentioned the important grief stage of anger, though I am certain all of them experienced anger at some point. Cindy Lou appeared to be the one most in touch with and able to label her feelings: "I saw my sinful life—outward. I didn't know about inward sin yet. I hated my life. Wanted church. I felt dirty, sinful, ugly. I wanted that to change." She went to a Christian church with a friend and realized that "Mormonism was not true." As she says, "And I was very angry. For three years, I was very angry. I felt like I had been betrayed, and I wanted to strike out at every Mormon that I saw."

Cindy Lou also experienced much fear. As she said, "I was scared to death of everything. I was a single mom. With my parents, I always knew that if I had financial problems, they would be there. Now, all of a sudden, what if I had financial problems? What if I couldn't feed my family? What if my car broke down? What would happen . . . ? But nothing happened."

Some converts had little fear in telling their family members of their decisions, but many got unexpected responses. For example, with Tawna Robinson, it was her non-Mormon father whose opinion carried the most weight. "I was denying my parents. I had been the perfect child. I had never gone against what they had wanted, and especially my father. There had been an abiding trust between us." Tawna told them about her decision to become a Christian. Although her mother cried and screamed, her father's re-

113

sponse was the more devastating: "But my father just shook his head. He was so disappointed. He said, 'I always thought you were more like me and didn't need religion. I see religion [as] your mother's crutch. Your mother needs that. But I thought you were strong.' He could not have hurt me more deeply than to say that he was disappointed. I was crushed."

Psychotherapists often define depression as anger turned inward. That may have been the case with Christine Campbell, who experienced massive depression at leaving the LDS church. For Christine the Lord used the *Course in Miracles* (a New Age book, purportedly channeled from Christ)[3] to first get Christine's attention. Christine spoke about that opportunity. "At about four months into the *Course in Miracles,* a friend invited me to a Women's Aglow meeting. Throughout the *Course in Miracles* I had not said aloud 'Christ' or 'Jesus.'" Attending that Women's Aglow meeting produced Christine's conversion experience, which I discussed earlier.

Tim Schmall's process of leaving the LDS church and coming to the Christian faith was complicated by his use of drugs. Tim (who wanted to speak with the number one God) started using drugs at the age of eleven. At this age, he learned about hypocrisy. "The same people I was going to church with I was doing drugs with." Tim tried not to be a hypocrite. "I came to church with a pack of cigarettes in my pocket." His on-again, off-again relationship with drugs mirrored his ambivalence toward the LDS church. At one point, when he was in high school, he said, "I'm going to stop doing all these drugs and straighten up. I'm going to do what God wants me to do." His bishop mapped out a course for him, including reading the Book of Mormon. This brought up questions that his seminary (week-day religion classes for adolescents) teacher could not answer to Tim's satisfaction. "I started becoming more familiar with the Bible, and as I did, things just didn't add up."

As Tim said, "The Lord was revealing to me—his spirit was witnessing to me—the truth. Then I started reading anti-Mormon literature. That really brought up some questions. . . . I started asking more questions, and I got less answers." Tim reported that he got so confused that he just pushed everything away. "My entire worldview, my philosophy of being, everything was crumbling. I was teetering. I was faltering. I didn't have any solid ground to stand on. I could not determine what the truth was." He went back to drugs. For his next attempt at recovery from his drug addiction, he went into the Marines. That story was told earlier.

We've heard a collection of stories that reveal the transitioning experiences of questioning Mormons. It is my hope that you have some sense of the difficulties people experience when leaving the LDS church and coming to historical Christianity.

The last chapter of this book is addressed to non-Mormon or never-Mormon Christians, those who, having found spiritual peace in their own lives, have naturally wanted to share their discovery with others. You are welcome to read further, but please notice this change in focus.

To the Traditional Christian Reader

I know this book will be of interest to traditional Christian readers who want to understand the process that their questioning Mormon friends, neighbors, fellow congregants, and parishioners are experiencing. This portion of the book, therefore, is addressed to them.

I asked the pastors interviewed what mistakes they had made in witnessing to Mormons. I also asked former Mormons who had come to know the biblical Jesus, "What mistakes, if any, did Christians make in trying to influence you?" The mistake most often identified involved the use of rational argument. The responses of both groups are included here.

The responses of two former Mormons, Sandra Tanner and Ross Anderson, have been included with those of the ministers. Sandra has a ministry to former Mormons and those thinking about leaving the LDS church. Ross is the pastor of an Evangelical Free church in Roy, Utah.

Ministers

With Ross, thinking through all the evidence in a rational way led to his decision to leave the LDS church. "So I thought that would be the approach that was going to work for everybody—stack up books, the documentation. I remember going through a series of propositions with my dad. He would agree with proposition number one, proposition number two, agree, agree, agree. Come to the obvious conclusion, and he's going, 'No.' So I was astounded that this didn't work. Just put the evidence on the table and they will be compelled to reject Mormonism." It doesn't work that way, of course.

Upon reflection, Pastor Ross offered, "What I've learned since—the other factor, in my experience, that I hadn't realized was so important was that [I had] a relationship with someone I trusted, that I valued enough to risk listening to what they had to say." He now offers this advice: "Preliminarily, I would try to build relationships and credibility. That's a long process. Their defenses are so strong."

Sandra Tanner also reminisced about her errors: "I became rabid to make my family see the truth. I was going at it tooth and nail and causing more problems than if I had not been so insistent that Mormonism was wrong. And what had I found? I was too aggressive, too demanding of them seeing what I had seen, not being sensitive to timing and to the Lord working on their heart. I had heard the truth, and I was going to nail them to the wall and make them hear also. . . . It took a while to get balanced more on the attitude of love. It wasn't coming across to people that I cared about them. It only came across that I wanted to be right and I wanted to win." She spoke about the ministry in her bookstore: "Early on I had to win with every Mormon that came in here. Now I don't have to have the last word. I can let them bear their testimony. I am much more willing to let the Holy Spirit do the convincing."

Pastor Pat Edwards agreed: "The idea that we can present them with objective truth, and they'll fall down on their knees and admit [the evidence is] right and change [was dominant]. Objective truth has nothing to do with Mormon belief system." Pat told a story about presenting contradictions between LDS doctrine and the Bible and getting this response: "You are increasing my faith, giving me these contradictions. It takes a lot of faith to believe in spite of them." Pat concluded, "That's our major error: If I know enough Mormon and biblical history, I can just present it to them, and they'll change. It just isn't so."

Pat also described the error of haste: "Believing that we can get a fairly quick response in our witnessing efforts, that we don't have to involve ourselves in their lives. We really have to become friends with these people whether they change or not. . . . Don't give up on friendship."

When asked about the mistakes he's made in trying to reach Mormons, Pastor Chris Vlachos answered in a similar way: "Thinking that my main goal was trying to get the Mormon to realize that Mormonism is false. . . . That my main task is to disprove Mormonism—historically, doctrinally." But Chris insisted, "It's a bad thing to do, because our main goal isn't to show the person that it's false. It's to show the person that he's a sinner, i.e., morally bankrupt in the presence of the holy and righteous God, and that Christ is the only provision to cover that sin. That's the goal."

Chris added, "Another mistake Christians make is to argue grace versus works—Ephesians versus James. Rather than argue with them, I'll basically shove them off in that direction—in the sense of Paul in Romans 2 and 3, add a few bricks to their pack, weights to prepare them for grace." He used the example of a man he had witnessed to in this way: "If you're going to come to God on the basis of works, you have to keep the law. You need to do this and this and this." Chris said the man told him that "I was the only one who had approached him that way—approaching him with works."

Chris commented on other mistakes, such as "putting Mormons on the defensive. . . . They have such a persecution complex that I like to let them take the initiative. . . . I don't give them the privilege of using, 'You're persecuting me,' because I let them start it first."

Pastor Bill Heersink said he made the mistake of "assuming things too quickly, for example, that all Latter-day Saints are the same." He also noted his difficulty in determining how confrontational to be. "I've erred on both sides, but probably more often on not being confrontive enough. If I take time to listen first and then avoid making it a personal attack, I find I can be quite direct."

And Pastor Jeff Silliman, too, was candid about his mistakes: "Being too harsh. Pushing too hard. . . . My biggest problem is to get Mormon folk who want to know me well enough that I can relate to them. A pastor! They are afraid."

Converts to Traditional Christianity

The Christian converts from the LDS church discussed their difficulties in accepting traditional Christianity, problems precipitated by the behavior of Christians in their lives.

Tawna Robinson said she had a problem with Christians "pressuring me to leave the Mormon church." After she accepted the Lord, members of Campus Crusade wanted her out there witnessing immediately. She found it difficult to stand her ground against that pressure as well. She wanted

120

time to grow in her new relationship with Jesus. She didn't always have success in setting boundaries.

Niki Payne had some valuable observations about the effect Christians had on her at the time of her conversion to the LDS church. "When I first joined the LDS church, Christians tried to argue doctrinal differences. But the arguments fell on deaf ears, because I was willing to believe that God had revealed new truth to Joseph Smith. It would have been more helpful to have been shown a broader view of what Christianity is and does versus what LDS doctrine does in terms of the very nature and definition of love, the nature of man's relationship to God, the nature of God's kingdom and his power on earth, as opposed to human authority and organizational power."

On the other hand, Niki mentioned, "The most helpful thing that Christians did to influence me was to simply express their own convictions about God's presence in their lives. Any attempt to proselytize was mistrusted by me as a Mormon because of my belief that those outside the church were corrupt and inferior. But a Christian expression of personal faith and belief was hope for me that perhaps Mormonism was not the only access to God, and that perhaps my fear that I would be corrupted was unfounded—that perhaps Mormonism was shortsighted, perhaps corrupt."

I did not ask those who identified themselves as Mormons what mistakes were made by Christians, but Wayne offered a comment about his cousin, who is an evangelical Christian. Wayne said that they have had long conversations about the historical gospel. Wayne has not been convinced. "I would have to have an experience like hers to believe." So far, the experience hasn't come.

Employing rational argument appears to be the major error made by traditional Christians when witnessing to Mormons, particularly when that argument is used to attack belief. Christians may feel it is a life and death matter to bring a Mormon to understanding, but they must not act as if it is. Mormons view their own beliefs as life and death matters. Christians must go gently.

What Christians Can Do

The pastors I interviewed used a variety of methods to integrate former Mormons into their congregations. I would not criticize any of these, but many former Mormons have great difficulty finding a home in Christian congregations. Some try to take Christ back with them to the familiarity of the LDS church. Pastors need to understand that it takes most former Mormons about five years to acclimate.[1] This may aggravate and intimidate pastors.

If interested congregants or pastors want to keep former Mormons in traditional Christian congregations, they can best serve these converts by providing a support group, led by the pastor or his staff, or referring the converts to one outside the congregation.

In my experience, many Mormons do not respond positively to rational arguments regarding errors either in the LDS gospel or in the history of their church. Most feel attacked. If the LDS church is part of their identity, they will defend it and silently judge their attacker as lacking understanding. There is strong resistance in Salt Lake City to the "evangelical movement," which is perceived as an uninformed attack on LDS church members by people unaware of the issues with which disaffected Mormons are grappling. We need patience while the questioning or inactive Mormon gains a listening ear.

Since most Mormons do not have an understanding of Christian doctrine and believe that the LDS church just has "additional information" beyond traditional Christian doctrine, I say to them simply, "But we believe in different gods and a different Jesus." Then I let them ask the questions.

While the books that argue rationally against Mormonism helped me refresh my understanding of the Mormon "gospel," I believe they will positively affect only those Mormons who are already questioning Mormonism and, therefore, in the process of leaving the LDS church. These books are valuable in clearing up the many questions regarding the differences between LDS doctrine and traditional Christianity. But if questioning Mormons read them too early, these potential converts may be startled by the information and return to their familiar culture and belief.

One book, Janis Hutchinson's *Out of the Cults and into the Church,* gives helpful guidance for both pastors and former Mormons. Hutchinson gives marvelous instructions for developing new Christian memories and a new cultural system.[2] The formation of both must be a conscious process by Mormons, pastors, and friends to replace the fear and disconnection that many former Mormons feel. Awareness of the Mormon cultural identity is necessary in order to understand what former Mormons are giving up. Books recommended for further reading are listed in the bibliography.

I learned a valuable lesson from another book I read, albeit not the lesson intended by the author. I used a technique this author recommended on a Mormon, a very close friend with whom I had been sharing conversations about doctrinal issues for over two years. The technique was merely to say, "I worry about you spending eternity in outer darkness." It backfired. She bolted right out of my life. Oh, if only we didn't learn our best lessons through painful experiences!

This experience stresses the fact that we shouldn't say anything that does not arise naturally out of our relationship with a person and out of love. When witnessing to Mormons, it also helps to remember that God is in charge, that it is he who will soften the heart of the listener, and that it is the witnessing person's job to be in relationship with the Mormon, as God is in relationship within the Trinity and with the Christian.

The answers given by the respondents are cause for introspection and prayer. They should also remind us that our knowledge is still incomplete, that we are all sinners, and that Christ died on the cross to wipe away those sins, bring us into permanent relationship with him, and grant us everlasting life.

Personally, conducting this research and writing this book has been a most rewarding and worthwhile experience, partly because I was able to confront my own Mormon roots. For example, on the ride home from an interview, I would be deluged by anti-Christian thoughts. I would entertain the notion that I was apostate to the "one true church" and would feel paralyzed with fear. I would try to find an understanding listener, but there was no one in my circle of acquaintances who could understand what I was talking about and could be compassionate. My former spiritual director looked at me in the midst of one of these fits with a condescending smile and said, "I don't understand what your problem is. It's no more difficult for a Mormon to come to the Lord than for anyone else." Maybe it is not more difficult for a Mormon than for anyone else, but Mormons do experience peculiar difficulties.

I would try to go over the points I knew were false in Mormonism, but most often I would come home and immerse myself in one of my truth-revealing books about the LDS church until the attacks stopped. My episodes of fear and confusion have diminished in intensity and content. It seems that being alone with this material provided an opportunity for me to reinvestigate the truth of the LDS church.

The greatest value for me in researching and writing this book was standing in the presence of God and the magnificence of his work in people's lives—both others' and my own.

Appendix A

A Letter from a Former Mormon

June 11, 1994

Dear Sandra Tanner and Ken Mulholland,

I just came from the Saturday morning session of the U.I.B.S. seminar. I particularly enjoyed your presentation, Sandra! As always, you touched my heart and enlightened my mind! May God bless you and Gerald! and keep you always in His loving care! Yours is such a VITAL mission and you do it so wonderfully well!

For the most part I very much enjoyed my experience! Except for hearing from David Crump, "Father, WE are very messed up people!" Personally, I find that remark very offensive! I should think that any person with a whit of self-worth would do likewise! God has helped me through so many things, to a point where I feel very good about who and what I am! I AM PROUD OF ME! I LIKE/LOVE ME! I TRULY BELIEVE THAT GOD IS/DOES ALSO! I BELIEVE THAT HE EXPECTS ME TO FEEL THE WAY I DO! Please tell "Dr. Crump" to speak for himself!

I attended Scott McKinney's workshop. I enjoyed it and found him to be very sincere, personable and knowledgeable. I was, however, very disappointed in the answer he gave to the questions I posed to him for the Q & A portion of the session:

1. From whence comes your authority?
2. Why is it superior to/greater than that of Mormonism?
3. Why are there so many widely (WILDLY!) varied Christian churches? How do you identify the 'real thing'?

To which I add one more: Because of the disparities and variances in the churches of the Christian realm, WHO HAS and WHAT IS the REAL TRUTH? HOW CAN I KNOW FOR ABSOLUTE CERTAIN?

I received what I felt was rather a non-answer to question #1: "That he was "CHOSEN" and given "SPECIAL GIFTS AND TALENTS." Come on now! Does anyone believe that good ol' Joe Smith did not possess "SPECIAL GIFTS AND TALENTS." (He is still conning the world, long after his death!) And he also believed or at least purported to be "CHOSEN"! And all of the little upstart Christian churches? I am sorry my mind does not buy it! Where does it begin? I require tangible verification that organized religion is truly OF AND BY GOD! Not just contrived by and for man! As I look at religion, in all its forms, so much seems so contrived to suit personal desires and agendas! So much is a matter of individual personal interpretation!

In my mind, GOD'S TRUTH IS CONSTANT! IT IS UNCHANGING BECAUSE IT IS ETERNAL TRUTH! IT DOES NOT WAIVER [sic]! IT WOULD NOT VARY FROM ONE RELIGION TO ANOTHER, OR EVEN FROM ONE CONGREGATION TO ANOTHER WITHIN THE SAME RELIGION! I am sorry, but the disparities and wide variances in the Christian churches makes me NUTS!

Before I proceed, I pray that you will receive this message in the exact same spirit it is presented! I am without guile! I am simply very frustrated and confused! I pray that you will be able to provide for me answers to questions that for many years now have eluded me! To answer what has been, for me, totally "UNANSWERABLE"!

Let me provide you some insight into who I am. I was born into Mormonism and practiced it for over thirty-five years. I held a multitude of very responsible positions. I was the "perfect" Mormon (MORON!) wife. Ours was the "perfect" Mormon family, until my oldest son began to resent being forced into blind obedience and servitude! He posed to me some very impressive and thought-provoking questions regarding Mormonism and was not content with the standard pat answers I provided (having learned them well!). His questions and the discussions they provoked started me seriously thinking!

Then our family was thrown into a situation with a bishop that tore our family from its very roots and destroyed it! That experience destroyed any and all belief I ever had as to the truthfulness of Mormonism and the divinity of its leaders! All of whom believe and/or purport to be "CHOSEN" and given "SPECIAL GIFTS AND TALENTS"!

If, as Christianity claims, and I agree, the Book of Mormon, D & C, Pearl of G. P., etc., are nothing more than a big fraud, who is to know the absolute validity of the Bible, with all its contradictions and inconsistencies? How can it be proven that it is anything more than a composite of "STORIES," BY MAN! FOR MAN! USED TO GOVERN AND CONTROL HUMAN BEHAVIOR?

Look at the discovery, very recently, regarding the speeches and writings of Boyd K. Packer,[1] Mormon authority. I remember, on many occasions, being totally mesmerized by the man's stories! Who can prove that the Bible is not merely a collection of such stories, passed down, changed, embellished, and expounded upon to suit conditions and needs at given points in time! If it is the true word of God, why the need for the changes and revisions that have taken place over the ages?

Since leaving Mormonism, feeling so horribly duped and betrayed, I have been very wary of organized religion, in all its forms! I have searched out many, many churches! I can find nothing in any of them to set them apart! In which I can place my absolute faith and trust! If Mormonism is such a farce, and yet Christianity parallels it in so many ways, who is to be believed and trusted? Is religion perhaps truly the opiate of the masses, as I've heard it said?

How can the Jimmy Swaggarts, Jerry Falwells, Oral Roberts, the Jimmy and Tammy Fay Bakers [sic] be explained away? Are they any more honorable or less evil and fraudulent than the Mormons? Those are but a few of the more recent and obvious examples that come to mind! One of the ugliest similarities I see between Mormonism and the Christian world is the puffed up, smug, self-righteous "We have it right—they are all wrong" attitude! It seems to me that NONE have [sic] it right or there would not be the disparities and variances between Christian religions, and even between congregations within the same religion! GOD'S TRUTH DOES NOT CHANGE ACCORDING TO THE WHIMS OF A GROUP OR A CERTAIN PASTOR! How can beliefs and values be altered so casually? I do not understand!

I am not for a minute defending Mormonism! I merely want to avoid the same pitfalls! I find it highly offensive and yet amusing that Christianity is steeped in and guilty of some of the very things they condemn Mormonism for!

I WOULD SO WELCOME THE SENSE OF BEING AND BELONGING SO MANY FIND IN RELIGION! The very reason I have searched out so many churches! and religions! I just have not found one in which I dare place my absolute trust and faith! Until I do, my religion must remain one-on-one with God my Father and Creator! The one religious truth in which I can place absolute faith and trust, without reservation, is that

I have a very loving Father and Creator who loves me UN-CONDITIONALLY! Who is ALWAYS there for me! Who NEVER fails me!

As I said, I pray that you will open your hearts and be receptive of the message as it comes from deep within my heart and soul! I am so frustrated! Surely, I am not alone in this! All I ask is for help to find answers to end the frustration and confusion I have endured for so many years! I know what I ask is not an easy thing! But I have not been able to do it alone! And God has not seen fit to guide me to any religion or church! Maybe this is what it will take!

Appendix B

Questionnaire

1. How old are you?
2. What sex?
3. How long have you been a Christian? Where do you worship? Do you have any responsibilities there? If so, please list them. Do you believe that the Bible is the Word of God and accept Jesus Christ as your personal Savior?
4. How long were you a Mormon? When were you baptized? Have you been to the temple? Did you hold any positions or responsibilities in the LDS church? Did you go on a mission?
5. When did you begin questioning the Church of Jesus Christ of Latter-day Saints? How old were you?
6. If you were asked to list specific steps in your leaving the LDS church, what would these be? (These may be both "internal" and "external," e.g., interior changes or exterior events. You may want to jot them down.)
7. Did you experience any costs, pains, or losses in leaving Mormonism? If so, what were they?
8. Does anything help compensate for these pains or losses? If so, what and how?

9. What were the hardest Mormon gospel doctrines to give up? Elaborate, please.

10. What were the most difficult Christian doctrines to accept? Elaborate, please.

11. What was the most difficult or painful life-changing aspect, if any, of your leaving the LDS church? Elaborate, please.

12. How and when did you begin to seek other ways of relating to God?

13. What mistakes, if any, did Christians make in trying to influence you?

14. Is there anything else you want to say?

15. Dr. Houston, my research professor, suggested that I ask: What was the most convincing and personally intimate need met by your conversion?

Appendix C

Results of Laura Marwick's Research

What follows is a synopsis of the research Laura Marwick conducted for her master's thesis from Brigham Young University.[1] Marwick examined several notable works, two of which were written by Russell Berg. Berg wrote two articles dealing with the reasons that Protestants become Catholics and vice versa.[2] Marwick drew parallels between Catholicism and the LDS church because each claims to be "the one true church," each has an authoritarian structure with the power to excommunicate, and each has as its main focus something or someone other than Jesus Christ. Additionally, both are male dominated. Marwick noted, "Both churches emphasize the divisions among the Protestants as evidence for disunity and legitimacy in claims of having the truth."[3]

Berg noted several reasons for persons to switch from Catholicism to Protestantism. Among them are spiritual dissatisfaction, lack of freedom to question or think for themselves, and, upon reading the Bible, perceived contradictions between Catholicism and biblical teaching or contradictions within Catholicism itself. These reasons are very similar to those revealed by my research with Mormons. It is of note that Berg's articles were published in 1959 and 1960. As Marwick noted in her thesis, "Berg's research was conducted in the 1950s and therefore, does not describe contemporary Catholicism. Post Vatican II Catholicism has placed more emphasis on Bible reading than it had previously and efforts to democratize parish and diocese life has created more space for independent thinking and questioning."[4] Such is not the case in the LDS church.

Another group of writers, S. L. Albrecht, M. Cornwall, and P. H. Cunningham, took a look at Mormon leave-taking and noted reasons that were similar to those my research revealed. Some of the former Mormons reported that they were uncomfortable with the emphasis on the Book of Mormon and "subsequently joined a church where the Bible was emphasized."[5] As Marwick pointed out, "Some Mormons who disaffiliate feel a spiritual lack within Mormonism which causes them to seek elsewhere for fulfillment. Many Mormons believe they are taught to follow the teachings and counsel of their leaders as right and true and not to question. This leads some who disaffiliate to perceive a restriction on their freedom to think and question. And finally many who disaffiliate perceive discrepancies within Mormonism and between Mormon teachings and the teachings of the Bible."[6]

Writing about Janet Jacobs's observations, Marwick stated, "She presents a model of deconversion in three stages: first, severing ties to the religious group; second, severing ties to the charismatic leader; and third, total separation from the movement and the redefinition of social reality."[7] These are all difficult stages to accomplish.[8] "The first stage of disobedience and rejection of the local authority . . . is much easier than admitting that you don't believe in the Prophet [refers to both the current prophet, the president of the LDS Church, and the original prophet, Joseph Smith]. Often, the Mormon feels a strong sense of love and devotion to the Prophet and has a difficult time rejecting him even after rejecting the doctrine and authority of the Church."[9]

Helen Rose Ebaugh is another writer who described the process of leaving, in this case leaving her role as a Catholic nun. She listed the stages as first doubts, seeking and weighing alternatives to her current role in the religious organization, turning points, and establishing an "ex-role identity."[10] By "ex-role identity" Ebaugh meant finding a new identity outside of her previous role in the religious organization. Wright, who wrote about leaving a cult, described the final stage of disaffiliation as "the defector's acquisition of a new identity, lifestyle, and worldview."[11]

Marwick formed a composite synthesized model, modifying the seven "necessary and constellationally sufficient conditions"[12] posited by J. Lofland and R. Stark. This composite model is a synthesis of Lofland and Stark, Ebaugh, and Jacobs:

> A person must experience (1) acute tensions felt within a religious perspective (Lofland and Stark) (2) resulting in first doubts (Ebaugh) (3) which cause them to seek and weigh role alternatives (Ebaugh/Lofland and Stark) (4) coming to a turning point where they (Ebaugh/Lofland and Stark) (5) sever ties to the religious group and the religious leader (Jacobs) (6) and form affective bonds with the new group resulting in (Lofland and Stark) (7) total separation from the movement, severing extracult attachments (Jacobs/Lofland and Stark) (8) resulting in the formation of an ex role identity (Ebaugh) (9) the redefinition of society (Jacobs) (10) and intensive interaction with the new affiliation (Lofland and Stark).[13]

Marwick said that this model is for the most part consistent with her research. But it is my assertion that this cold and clinical approach takes all the wonder, the beauty, and the majesty out of God's workings in the lives of the people he brings into his kingdom. While the model is the result of valid research methods and the best of scientific thinking, it attempts to put God into a box. And he just doesn't fit.

In all fairness to Marwick, she did mention the diversity in the responses to her research:

> As with each of the separate models, the disaffiliation and conversion experience could be captured only in part by the synthesized model. There was such diversity and complexity among the sample that inevitably some of this is lost when all of the unique cases are condensed into a single model. The synthesized model did, however, accurately encompass a broad description of the disaffiliation and conversion experience of the subjects.[14]

Appendix D

Sandra Tanner's Transition Steps

Coming Out of LDS

1. Some minor doubts—pushed to the back of mind.
2. Challenged by a friend or book.
3. Start reading both sides. May even begin as effort to silence critics.
4. Growing awareness of depth of problems. Struggle with who to believe.
5. Growing anger over leaders' dishonesty.
6. Finally reject LDS leaders as inspired.
7. Distrust of other churches and ministers.
8. Fear of rejection by family.

Coming to Christ

1. Desire for something more from religion than activity.
2. Assume already following Bible (ignorance of true Christianity).
3. Meet some spiritual Christians or attend some meetings where God is truly glorified and worshiped.

4. A longing for that closer relationship to Christ we see in others.
5. Exposure to Bible doctrine.
6. Growing desire to square all beliefs with the Bible.
7. Look for place of worship or Bible study that truly points to Christ, not man.
8. Growing desire to have Christ as Lord of every area of life.

Notes

Preface to the Second Edition

1. See glossary for definition of *temple recommend*.

2. The myth of Mormonism is that the golden plates and other revelations are a fabrication of Joseph Smith's mind.

3. Fawn M. Brodie, *No Man Knows My History: The Life of Joseph Smith the Mormon Prophet* (New York: Alfred E. Knopf, 1945).

4. Being sealed with my husband meant, according to LDS doctrine, that we would be married for "time and eternity" and, with righteous living, have rights to populate our own worlds.

5. I could take much of my course work in Salt Lake City, which had a satellite location at the Utah Institute for Biblical Studies. I had to go to Canada only three times.

Introduction

1. Three such conferences were held in 1990, 1992, and 1994. UIBS, in conjunction with Sandra Tanner's Utah Lighthouse Ministries, produced them. They were staffed and attended by a nationwide (with the addition of Canada) group of people (about 120 to 150 annually), who have experience with the LDS church. They shared their successes and their failures in witnessing to Mormons and new information on Mormon history and doctrine.

2. The Utah Institute for Biblical Studies was founded in 1984 to provide quality theological education to Utah's laity. Beginning in 1998, UIBS will grant graduate degrees.

3. There are many definitions of *cult*. I will use Ruth A. Tucker's: "A 'cult' is a religious group that has a 'prophet'-founder called of God to give a special message not found in the Bible itself, often apocalyptic in nature and often set forth in 'inspired' writings. In deference to this charismatic figure or these 'inspired' writings, the style of leadership is authoritarian and there is frequently an exclusivistic outlook, supported by a legalistic lifestyle and persecution mentality" (*Another Gospel* [Grand Rapids: Zondervan, 1989], 16).

4. Janis has since assured me that many former Mormons have indeed benefited from reading her book and also stated a similar aversion to the term *cult* on the part of both former and current Mormons.

5. Laura M. Marwick, "From Mormon to Evangelical: A Look at Disaffiliation and Conversion" (master's thesis, Brigham Young University, 1994).

6. Leslie Reynolds, "God Works in Mysterious Ways" (ministry research project, Regent College, Vancouver, B.C., 1995).

7. A membership of 9,694,549 as of the end of 1996 was announced at the April 1997 general conference of the LDS church. Membership figures are released annually in April. Additionally, a press release from the public affairs division of the LDS church, dated February 26, 1996, stated that new members are being converted at a rate of 950 per day.

8. "But, behold, I say unto you, that you must study it out in your mind; then you must ask me if it be right, and if it is right I will cause that your bosom shall burn within you; therefore, you shall feel that it is right" (*Doctrine and Covenants* [Salt Lake City: The Church of Jesus Christ of Latter-day Saints, 1987]).

Chapter 1: Traditional Christianity versus Mormonism

1. I determined that she was angry based, in part, on the style of her letter, which was written in italics with numerous capital letters in bold and regular type, exclamation points almost exclusively as ending punctuation, and numerous underlinings. Because the letter was so difficult to read, I modified it to a more readable form. I have, therefore, deleted italics, underlines, and bold type.

2. Janis Hutchinson, *Out of the Cults and into the Church* (Grand Rapids: Kregel, 1994), 188.

3. Latayne C. Scott, *After Mormonism What?* (Grand Rapids: Baker, 1994), 22.

4. Jan Shipps, *Mormonism: The Story of a New Religious Tradition* (Chicago: University of Illinois Press, 1985), ix.

5. Ibid., x.

6. Ruth A. Tucker, *Another Gospel* (Grand Rapids: Zondervan, 1989), 49.

7. Ken Mulholland, "LDS Evangelism Seen as a Cross-Cultural Mission" (Salt Lake City: Utah Institute for Biblical Studies, 1991), 1.

8. *Gospel Principles* (Salt Lake City: The Church of Jesus Christ of Latter-day Saints, 1986), 354.

9. Milton R. Hunter, *Gospel through the Ages* (Salt Lake City: Stevens and Wallace, 1945), 104; and Charles W. Penrose, *Millennial Star* (Liverpool: Orson Pratt, n.d.), 181, both quoted in Gordan H. Fraser, *Is Mormonism Christian?* (Chicago: Moody Press, 1965), 43.

10. *Gospel Principles*, 65–66.

11. Apostle M. Russell Ballard, KUTV, "Take Two," interview by Rod Decker, Salt Lake City, 22 June 1997.

12. *Gospel Principles*, 9.

13. Ibid., 34.

14. Ibid., 234.

15. "The Articles of Faith of the Church of Jesus Christ of Latter-day Saints," *Pearl of Great Price* (Salt Lake City: The Church of Jesus Christ of Latter-day Saints, 1987), 60–61.

16. "The Mediator," *Ensign* (May 1977): 54–55, quoted in *Gospel Principles*, 69–71.

17. Ibid., 68.

18. Spencer W. Kimball, *The Miracle of Forgiveness* (Salt Lake City: Bookcraft, 1969), 325.

19. James R. White, *Letters to a Mormon Elder* (Southbridge, Mass.: Crowne Publications, 1990), 352–53.

20. *Gospel Principles*, 100–101.

21. "The Articles of Faith of the Church of Jesus Christ of Latter-day Saints," 60–61.

Chapter 2: Needs Unmet by Mormonism

1. Janis Hutchinson, *Out of the Cults and into the Church* (Grand Rapids: Kregel, 1994), 191.

2. In fairness, I include a comment by a Presbyterian proofreader: "I'm wondering about some of the blind faith issues and 'put off' responses. I really think most religions have them too, especially for young people. ('God knows; we don't. We can't understand how God works because we're only human; that's something you have to accept on faith.'

These are all responses I got to questions as a child.) How many folks in any congregation are bright enough to grapple with the philosophy of religion?"

3. This story is detailed in several fascinating books. See, for example, Robert Lindsey, *A Gathering of Saints* (New York: Dell Publishing, 1988).

4. Sterling M. McMurrin, interview in the now defunct *Seventh East Press,* quoted in Robert Lindsey, *A Gathering of Saints* (New York: Dell Publishing, 1988), 103.

Chapter 3: Motivations to Question Further

1. H.I.S. stands for "high school interdenominational studies," which is now a part of the Christian Network of Utah. McGarvey is the president of CYN.

Chapter 4: Criticism from within the LDS Church

1. David Johnson et al., *The Subtle Power of Spiritual Abuse* (Minneapolis: Bethany House, 1991), 88.

2. As *Time* magazine's August 4, 1997, cover story on the LDS church points out, church leaders are picked for their success in the temporal world, rather than for their theological or pastoral care abilities or training.

3. Ronald M. Enroth, *Churches That Abuse* (Grand Rapids: Zondervan, 1992), 31.

4. The public information office of the LDS church neither confirmed nor denied the existence of such a study. Their spokesperson merely said, "These studies are done only for our internal use. They are not released to the public."

5. Janis Hutchinson, *Out of the Cults and into the Church* (Grand Rapids: Kregel, 1994), 128.

6. Ibid.

Chapter 5: Healing the Wounds

1. Sir Richard, who traveled the world and wrote during the mid-1800s, came to

Utah and authored a book about that experience, *The City of the Saints,* published in London in 1861.

2. Ruth Tucker, *Another Gospel* (Grand Rapids: Zondervan, 1989), 319.

Chapter 6: Those Captured by Christianity

1. An anti-Mormon videotape, about which the Christian Book Distributors catalogue says, "With an investigation into the pagan temple rituals and interviews with leaders in the cult, this controversial film reveals the heartbreaking accounts of families and lives destroyed by the Mormon church and its heretical beliefs and practices."

2. The four laws result in the following four actions:
   1. Admit your need (I am a sinner).
   2. Be willing to turn from your sins (repent).
   3. Believe that Jesus Christ died for you on the cross and rose from the grave.
   4. Through prayer, invite Jesus Christ to come in and control your life through the Holy Spirit (receive him as Lord and Savior).

Taken from "Steps to Peace with God" (Minneapolis: The Billy Graham Evangelistic Association).

Chapter 7: A Change in Worldview

1. The eighth of thirteen LDS Articles of Faith states, "We believe the Bible to be the word of God as far as it is translated correctly; we also believe the Book of Mormon to be the word of God." Taken from "The Articles of Faith of the Church of Jesus Christ of Latter-day Saints," *Pearl of Great Price* (Salt Lake City: The Church of Jesus Christ of Latter-day Saints, 1987), 60.

2. The Book of Mormon is in its wording (but not in Mormon interpretation of those words) much closer to the Bible than other Mormon "scriptures." Joseph Smith's new doctrine is presented in the *Doctrine and*

Covenants and the *Pearl of Great Price,* in the second of which he begins to give a new "translation" of the Bible.

3. Utah Institute for Biblical Study is located at 232 University, Salt Lake City, UT 84102.

4. The Reorganized Church of Jesus Christ of Latter-day Saints was formed early in the Mormon experience, shortly after the death of Joseph Smith when the LDS church split into two factions. One of the major points of contention was the process of picking a new prophet. The Reorganized Church maintained that the position should be kept in Smith's blood line.

5. Gode Davis, "Closet Addictions, Utah Women Hooked on Prescription Drugs," *Network* 12, no. 8 (November 1989): 16. *Network* is a Salt Lake weekly news and feature magazine.

6. Janis Hutchinson, *Out of the Cults and into the Church* (Grand Rapids: Kregel, 1994), 194.

Chapter 8: Additional Experiences

1. Mormons believe that at death nonbelievers go to a paradise, where they have an opportunity to accept the gospel. If their "temple work" (that is, baptism, marriage, etc.) was done by someone here on earth, they will be eligible for the celestial kingdom. A major portion of the temple work is done by using stand-ins for the dead and performing these ceremonies.

2. Utah Lighthouse Ministries, P.O. Box 1884, Salt Lake City, UT 84110.

3. The *Course in Miracles* is a New Age book purportedly channeled by Jesus through a professor of medical psychology at Columbia University named Helen Shucman. (*A Course in Miracles* [Glen Ellen, Calif.: Foundation for Inner Peace, 1975].) The book contains three sections: (1) Text, (2) Workbook for Students, and (3) Manual for Teachers. (It was in the second year of doing the rigorous daily meditations prescribed in the book that I was brought to the Lord. I,

like Christine, barely acknowledged the words *Jesus* or *Christ* and certainly never spoke them aloud.)

Chapter 9: To the Traditional Christian Reader

1. Janis Hutchinson says it takes three to eight years to successfully make the transition from Mormonism to traditional Christianity. *Out of the Cults and into the Church* (Grand Rapids: Kregel, 1994), 30.

2. Hutchinson, in her book *Out of the Cults and into the Church,* gives examples of building new Christian memories in former Mormons. As a sociologist, she also gives many useful tips for counseling former Mormons.

Appendix A: A Letter from a Former Mormon

1. The letter writer may mean Paul Dunn.

Appendix C: Results of Laura Marwick's Research

1. Laura M. Marwick, *From Mormon to Evangelical: A Look at Disaffiliation and Conversion* (Provo, Utah: Brigham Young University, 1994).

2. Russell O. Berg, "Why Protestants Become Catholics?" *Christian Herald,* and "Why Catholics Become Protestants?" *Christian Herald,* 1960, quoted in Marwick, *From Mormon to Evangelical,* 19.

3. Marwick, *From Mormon to Evangelical,* 22–23.

4. A. M. Greeley, *The Catholic Myth: The Behavior and Beliefs of American Catholics* (New York: Charles Scribners, 1990), quoted in Marwick, *From Mormon to Evangelical,* 23.

5. S. L. Albrecht, M. Cornwall, and P. H. Cunningham, "Religious Leave Taking: Disengagement and Disaffiliation among Mormons," in *Falling from the Faith,* ed. D. G. Bromley (Rye, N.Y.: Sage Publications, 1988), 77.

6. Marwick, *From Mormon to Evangelical,* 24–25.

7. Janet Jacobs, *Divine Disenchantment* (Bloomington, Ind.: University Press, 1989), 38, quoted in Marwick, *From Mormon to Evangelical,* 30.

8. With respect to Mormonism and this process, see Janis Hutchinson, *Out of the Cults and into the Church* (Grand Rapids: Kregel, 1994).

9. Marwick, *From Mormon to Evangelical,* 31.

10. H. R. F. Ebaugh, *Becoming an Ex* (Chicago: University of Chicago Press, 1989), 34, quoted in Marwick, *From Mormon to Evangelical,* 33–34.

11. S. Wright, "Leaving Cults: The Dynamics of Defection," Society for the Scientific Study of Religion. Monograph Series, Number 7, 73.

12. J. Lofland and R. Stark, "Becoming a World Saver: A Theory of Conversion to a Deviant Perspective," *American Sociological Review* 30, no. 874, quoted in Marwick, *From Mormon to Evangelical,* 35.

13. Marwick, *From Mormon to Evangelical,* 42.

14. Ibid., 94.

Glossary

Many of these definitions were written after consulting *Gospel Doctrine* published by the Church of Jesus Christ of Latter-day Saints, *Why We Left Mormonism* by Latayne Scott, and *Speaking the Truth in Love to Mormons* by Mark J. Cares, with permission.

Adam-god doctrine. LDS: Early teachings by Brigham Young and others that identified Adam as being God.

Aaronic priesthood. LDS: The lesser of the two divisions in the priesthood in the LDS church. It serves as the entry point into the priesthood for boys twelve and older and adult male converts. The offices of the Aaronic priesthood are deacon, teacher, and priest.

accepting Jesus. Christian: Acknowledging Jesus as a person's personal Lord and Savior.

Adam. LDS: One of Heavenly Father's finest spirit children. He was sent to earth to make man mortal, which he accomplished through his fall. Before his earthly life, he led the righteous in the war in heaven. He helped in the creation of the earth. Christian: The first man, who was tempted by his wife and disobeyed God's commands, bringing sin and therefore death into the world.

agency. LDS: A person's free will and natural capacity to choose either good or evil. Christian: The Bible teaches that mankind by nature is spiritually dead and thoroughly evil, that is, preferring its judgments and opinions to God's commands.

apostasy. LDS: (1) The act of leaving the LDS church. (2) Also the "Great Apostasy," the time between the separation of the original apostles and Joseph Smith's establishment of the LDS church. Mormons teach that during this long period of time the true church was gone from the earth.

apostle. LDS: (1) Sometimes a reference to the original twelve apostles. (2) More often a reference to the twelve current apostles of the LDS church, who serve immediately under the First Presidency of the church.

Articles of Faith. LDS: Thirteen brief statements of faith that are part of the *Pearl of Great Price* and therefore are considered scripture.

authority. LDS: The right to function in certain capacities in the LDS church.

baptism for the dead. LDS: The belief that spirits who accept the LDS church in the spirit world cannot progress until they are baptized. Such spirits must receive baptism vicariously through a living person. Such baptisms can only be performed in an LDS temple.

bear testimony. LDS: A popular expression for testifying about the state of one's faith, often including the truth of the LDS church and the validity of Joseph Smith and the current prophet.

Bible. LDS: One of four books considered scripture. Believed to be the Word of God "as far as it is translated correctly." Christian: The Word of God.

bishop. LDS: The head of the local ward (congregation) for five to seven years. Bishops have no formal theological training. They have responsibility for the temporal and spiritual well-being of their ward members.

bishopric. LDS: A bishop and his two counselors.

Book of Abraham. LDS: A section of the *Pearl of Great Price,* and thus a part of LDS scripture. It describes gods creating the world and mentions Kolob, the planet closest to God's throne. Joseph Smith claimed to have translated it from Egyptian papyri he obtained. [In 1967 these papyri were found in the Metropolitan Museum in New York and determined by Egyptologists to be a description of burial rites.]

Book of Mormon. LDS: Subtitled "Another Testament of Jesus Christ," is one of four books considered scripture. It contains the story of the migrations of groups of Jews to the Americas and their subsequent history there.

Book of Moses. LDS: A section of the *Pearl of Great Price* and thus considered scripture. It contains teachings on the plurality of gods, Adam's "good" fall, and Satan's rebellion and fall.

Brigham Young. LDS: The second president of the church. After Joseph Smith's death, he led the Mormons to Utah, where they prospered under his leadership.

celestial kingdom. LDS: The highest of the three kingdoms of heaven. It in turn contains three levels, the highest of which is referred to as exaltation.

celestial marriage. LDS: Being married in the temple for time and eternity, which is essential for exaltation. It is also called eternal marriage. This ordinance can be performed vicariously for the dead.

confirmation. LDS: Brief ceremony following baptism in which a new member is instructed to receive the Holy Ghost.

deacon. LDS: The first office of the Aaronic priesthood. Worthy boys enter it at the age of twelve. Deacons help distribute the sacrament (Lord's Supper) in worship meetings. Christian: A service position in many traditional churches.

disfellowshiped. LDS: A judgment arrived at by a disciplinary council for serious sin. It is one step removed from excommunication. A disfellowshiped member loses privileges.

Doctrine and Covenants. LDS: One of the four books of scripture which records early revelations and official proclamations.

elder. LDS: Lowest office of the Melchizedek priesthood. Christian: A service position in many traditional churches.

eternal family. LDS: The earthly family unit that remains a family unit for all eternity and increases through the procreation of spirit children for all eternity by those who attain the celestial kingdom.

eternal progression. LDS: The belief that a person can continue to progress throughout eternity, eventually obtaining godhood.

exaltation. LDS: The highest level of the celestial kingdom, godhood.

excommunication. LDS: Excommunication is the most severe judgment an LDS disciplinary council can take, severing a member from the church. Christian: An act of severing a member from church performed in some churches.

fall of Adam. LDS: Change to mortality that occurred when Adam ate the forbidden fruit. Christian: The act that brought sin and therefore death into the world.

fast and testimony meeting. LDS: Held on the first Sunday of every month. Instead of having assigned speakers, any member can come forward and bear his or her testimony.

First Presidency. LDS: The president of the LDS Church and his two counselors.

first vision. LDS: The vision Joseph Smith received in 1820 when Heavenly Father told him not to join any church since they were all corrupt.

free salvation. Christian: Salvation is freely offered through the death of Jesus Christ on the cross.

General Authority. LDS: The title for a church leader whose authority is not limited to one geographical area but is general. The General Authorities consist of the First Presidency of the

Church, the Quorum of the Twelve Apostles, the First and Second Quorums of the Seventy, and the Presiding Bishopric.

general conference. LDS: Business and worship meetings held twice a year (April and October) in Salt Lake City.

gentile. LDS: A non-Mormon [includes Jews]. Christian: New Testament designation for other than Jews.

God. LDS: Our Heavenly Father, who was once a man who subsequently obtained godhead. He's therefore an exalted man with a physical body, the Father of Jesus Christ and of the spirits of all men. Christian: God is three persons, Father, Son (Jesus Christ), and the Holy Spirit, in the unity of one substance.

Godhead. LDS: The Father, Son, and Holy Ghost, three distinct beings.

godhood. LDS: The ultimate goal of a practicing member.

gospel. LDS: A common term for the teachings of the plan of salvation. It embraces all that is necessary to save and exalt mankind. Christian: The biblical message (Good News) of free and full salvation won for mankind by Jesus Christ.

grace. LDS: The power God gives people to save themselves, granted *only* after they have done everything they can do. Christian: The unconditional, undeserved, unfathomable love on God's part that moved him to save us.

high council. LDS: A council of twelve men on the stake level that assists the stake presidency.

high priest. LDS: The highest office of the Melchizedek priesthood, to which all General Authorities, bishoprics, stake presidencies, and patriarchs are ordained.

Holy Ghost. LDS: A member of the Godhead, the Holy Ghost does not have a body and is not equal to Heavenly Father.

Holy Spirit. Christian: One member of the Trinity equal with the Father, yet with a separate role.

institute. LDS: Theological instruction center for college students, near many college and university campuses. Formally, LDS Institute of Religion.

intelligence. LDS: The part of mankind that is eternal. Heavenly Father (pro)created spiritual bodies for intelligences to inhabit.

Jack Mormon. A slang expression for a nonactive Mormon.

Jesus. LDS: (1) The first spirit child of Heavenly Father. (2) Jehovah. (3) The only begotten Son—that is, the only child Heavenly Father physically begat on earth. (4) As the Savior, one (a) who conquered physical death for mankind, (b) who paid our debt and is patient with us as we repay that debt, and (c) who serves as our example, showing us what we have to do to save ourselves. Christian: A member of the Trinity, our Lord and Savior, Christ offered himself up on the cross at Calvary as payment for our sins.

John the Baptist. LDS: Appeared to Joseph Smith and Oliver Cowdery on May 15, 1829, and bestowed upon them the Aaronic priesthood.

Joseph Smith. The founder of the LDS religion and the first prophet, seer, and revelator.

justification. Christian: God's declaring us free from guilt on the basis of Christ's atoning work.

LDS. Abbreviation for Latter-day Saints.

Melchizedek priesthood. LDS: The higher priesthood that worthy young men enter at the age of eighteen or nineteen. The offices of the Melchizedek priesthood are elder, seventy, high priest, and patriarch.

mission. LDS: Worthy males serve a two-year mission at about age nineteen. They seek converts among Christians, not the unchurched.

missionary discussions. LDS: Six lessons missionaries present to investigators.

Mormon. Popular name for a member of The Church of Jesus Christ of Latter-day Saints. (All of those interviewed for this book referred to themselves as Mormons. They seldom used the term LDS in any form.)

Only Begotten Son. LDS: Refers to Jesus. The only person of whom Heavenly Father is the father of his mortal body. Christian: Jesus Christ.

outer darkness. LDS: Contains the devil and his followers. The closest LDS belief to the biblical concept of hell.

patriarchal blessing. LDS: An inspired blessing declaring a person's lineage and giving inspired counsel and insight about his or her life.

Pearl of Great Price. LDS: The smallest of the four Mormon scriptures, containing the Books of Moses, Abraham, and Joseph Smith, as well as the Articles of Faith.

plan of salvation. LDS: God's program for his children by which they can overcome sin and death and gain eternal life.

plurality of gods. LDS: Whereas there is a single God who is our creator, he is one among a number of gods in the universe.

plural marriage. LDS: The abandoned church practice commonly called polygamy. In 1843 this doctrine became part of LDS scripture. Plural marriage had been practiced by Joseph Smith and selected others previous to this and continued to be practiced openly until 1890. At that time, the church president, Wilford Woodruff, received a revelation that forbade this practice in the world. However, plural temple marriages, valid for eternity, but not for time on this earth, are still available for worthy male members.

president (of the church). LDS: The "prophet, seer, and revelator," or the living prophet. He alone receives direct revelations for the church as a whole.

priesthood. LDS: Entered into by all worthy male members. Defined as both the authority and power God gives to act on his behalf. Christian: A priesthood of all believers, although some clergy are called priests.

primary. LDS: A Sunday school-like organization for children ages three to eleven.

redeem the dead. LDS: One of the main missions of the LDS church. *See* baptism for the dead.

RLDS. Abbreviation for the Reorganized Church of Jesus Christ of Latter-day Saints, based in Independence, Missouri. After Joseph Smith's death, a faction of Mormons recognized Smith's son rather than Brigham Young as their leader and founded the RLDS church. To this day it is led by direct descendants of Joseph Smith.

sacrament. LDS: Used exclusively as a reference to the Lord's Supper, consisting of bread and water. Offered every Sunday.

sacrament meeting. LDS: Sunday church service. Auxiliary meetings are held on Sundays as well.

Satan. LDS: Heavenly Father's spirit child who proposed an alternate plan of salvation. After Heavenly Father rejected it, Satan rebelled. Heavenly Father sent him, along with his followers (demons), to outer darkness. This means that they lost forever their chance to obtain physical bodies and to continue their progression to godhood.

Savior. LDS: Jesus Christ, who paid humanity's debt to Heavenly Father and conquered death for mankind. This debt must be redeemed through obedience to God's commandments. Christian: Jesus Christ, who saved us fully and freely by paying for our sins, canceling our debt.

Scripture. LDS: Words, both written and spoken, by holy men of God when moved upon by the Holy Ghost. Christian: The written Word of God.

seminary. LDS: Week-day instruction on LDS doctrine and history offered to secondary school students. Christian: A postgraduate theological school.

Seventy. LDS: A title of an office in the Melchizedek priesthood devoted to mission work.

sons of perdition. LDS: Ex-Mormons who go to outer darkness in the hereafter and therefore lose the opportunity to progress. Those who know the truth and then later deny it.

soul. LDS: The essence of life, which includes the body. Christian: The essence or seat of life.

spirit children. LDS: In a preexistence everyone lived as a spirit child of Heavenly Father and Mother.

spirit prison. LDS: The section of the spirit world where non-Mormon spirits go after death. Spirits from paradise can convert the inhabitants of spirit prison.

stake. LDS: An organizational unit consisting of a number of wards.

stake president. LDS: The head of a stake, assisted by two counselors.

telestial kingdom. LDS: The lowest kingdom of heaven. It is not visited by Heavenly Father or Jesus but only by the Holy Ghost. This is the final destination of carnal and wicked people. Its glory is described as surpassing all mortal understanding.

temple. LDS: A consecrated place of worship and prayer. Only temple-worthy members in good standing can enter this house of the Lord, prepared and dedicated for sacred gospel ordinances. Christian: An Old Testament term for the house of the Lord.

temple recommend. LDS: A card declaring one "temple worthy" given after an extensive interview by one's bishop and stake president.

temple work. LDS: Participation in various temple ordinances, including baptism, marriage, and sealing, for the living and, vicariously, for the dead.

terrestrial kingdom. LDS: The middle kingdom of heaven, where people will be visited by Jesus but not by Heavenly Father. This is the final destination of honorable people and inactive members.

The Church of Jesus Christ of Latter-day Saints. The official name of the LDS church.

ward. LDS: A local LDS congregation, usually defined by geographical boundaries.

Word of Wisdom. LDS: Dietary principles that, among other things, rule out the use of alcohol, tobacco, and "hot drinks" (which have been officially interpreted as tea and coffee). A member must keep the Word of Wisdom to be temple worthy.

Bibliography

Recommended for Further Reading

Cares, Mark J. *Speaking the Truth in Love to Mormons.* Milwaukee: Northwestern Publishing Company, 1993.

Enroth, Ronald M. *Churches That Abuse.* Grand Rapids: Zondervan, 1992.

Hutchinson, Janis. *Out of the Cults and into the Church.* Grand Rapids: Kregel, 1994.

Johnson, David and J. VanVonderen. *The Subtle Power of Spiritual Abuse.* Minneapolis: Bethany House, 1991.

Scott, Latayne C. *After Mormonism What?* Grand Rapids: Baker, 1994.

———. *Why We Left Mormonism.* Grand Rapids: Baker, 1990.

Shipps, Jan. *Mormonism: The Story of a New Religious Tradition.* Chicago: University of Illinois Press, 1985.

Tanner, Jerald and Sandra. *The Changing World of Mormonism.* Chicago: Moody Press, 1981.

———. *Major Problems of Mormonism.* Salt Lake City: Lighthouse Ministry, 1989.

White, James R. *Letters to a Mormon Elder.* Southbridge, Mass.: Crowne Publications, 1990.

Of a Lighter Nature

Laake, Deborah. *Secret Ceremonies.* New York: William Morrow and Company, 1993.

Lindsey, Robert. *A Gathering of Saints.* New York: Dell Publishing, 1988.

Academic References

Albrecht, S. L., M. Cornwall, and P. H. Cunningham. "Religious Leave Taking: Disengagement and Disaffiliation Among Mormons." In *Falling from the Faith,* edited by D. G. Bromley. Newbury Park, N.J.: Sage Publications, 1988.

Ebaugh, H. R. F. *Becoming an Ex.* Chicago: University of Chicago Press, 1989.

Greeley, A. M. *The Catholic Myth: The Behavior and Beliefs of American Catholics.* New York: Charles Scribners, 1990.

Jacobs, Janet. *Divine Disenchantment.* Bloomington, Ind.: University Press, 1989.

Marwick, Laura M. *From Mormon to Evangelical: A Look at Disaffiliation and Conversion.* Provo, Utah: Brigham Young University, 1994.

Tucker, Ruth A. *Another Gospel.* Grand Rapids: Academie Books (Zondervan), 1989.

Vlachos, Chris. *Adam Is God?* Moscow, Idaho: Community Christian Ministries, 1979.

LDS References

Book of Mormon. Salt Lake City: The Church of Jesus Christ of Latter-day Saints, 1987.

Burton, D. Jeff. *For Those Who Wonder.* Bountiful, Utah: IVE, 1994.

Doctrine and Covenants. Salt Lake City: The Church of Jesus Christ of Latter-day Saints, 1987.

Gospel Principles. Salt Lake City: The Church of Jesus Christ of Latter-day Saints, 1986.

Kimball, Spencer W. *The Miracle of Forgiveness.* Salt Lake City: Bookcraft, 1969.

Pearl of Great Price. Salt Lake City: The Church of Jesus Christ of Latter-day Saints, 1987.

Dr. Leslie Reynolds, formerly a Mormon and psychotherapist, is a public speaker, an educator, and an advocate for the poor. She completed advanced studies at Loyola Marymount (M.A.T.), Columbia Pacific University (Ph.D. in counseling), and Regent College (M.C.S. in applied theology).